grieving
with hope

grieving
with hope

FINDING COMFORT
AS YOU JOURNEY
THROUGH LOSS

SAMUEL J. HODGES, IV
AND KATHY LEONARD

BakerBooks
a division of Baker Publishing Group
Grand Rapids, Michigan

© 2011 by Samuel J. Hodges IV and Kathy Leonard

Published by Baker Books
a division of Baker Publishing Group
P.O. Box 6287, Grand Rapids, MI 49516-6287
www.bakerbooks.com

Printed in the United States of America

Library of Congress Cataloging-in-Publication Data
Hodges, Samuel J., IV
    Grieving with hope : finding comfort as you journey through loss / Samuel J. Hodges IV and Kathy Leonard.
        p.   cm.
    ISBN 978-0-8010-1423-9 (pbk.)
    1. Consolation. 2. Grief—Religious aspects—Christianity. 3. Bereavement—Religious aspects—Christianity. I. Leonard, Kathy. II. Title.
BV4905.3.H63 2011
248.8′6—dc22   2011015407

Published in association with the literary agency of Credo Communications, LLC, Grand Rapids, Michigan 49525; www.credo communications.net.

19   20   21   22   23   14   13   12   11

Contents

Preface   7

1   What to Expect in Grief   9
2   Coping with Grief   18
3   Will This Pain Ever End?   26
4   Healthy Ways to Relieve Your Pain   32
5   Feeling Alone   42
6   Adjusting to Your New Reality   52
7   Dealing with Insensitive Comforters   61
8   Your Grieving Family   68
9   Making Sense of Your Situation   78
10   How Your Thinking Shapes Your Grief   85
11   Forgiving Those Responsible for the Death   92
12   Dealing with Regret and Guilt   99
13   Anger with God   107
14   What Grief Teaches Us   114

Contents

15 How Do I Get through This?   123

16 Grieving with Hope and Joy   132

Appendix A: Featured Experts   145

Appendix B: GriefShare®: Help for Those in Grief   151

Preface

You are to be commended for using the precious little energy you have to read this book, because if you're grieving the death of a loved one or friend, you may feel you cannot go on. Picking up a book to find strength is like trying to move your car from your garage to your driveway—by lifting it. Your emotions can be overwhelming. Questions and regrets may plague you. You may feel abandoned, alone, and deeply sad.

This book represents hundreds of hours of interviews with people who've experienced the death of a loved one, including Christian counselors and teachers and others who care for the bereaved. These people have been there, and they want to share how they made it through. Through their insights, you'll find out what to expect in the days to come, what to do with your emotions and your questions of "why," and how to get through the days when you feel you can't.

Most importantly, you will discover how to have hope and peace amid your heartache and pain. You don't have to walk this journey alone. As you'll see, others have made it through grief. You will too.

1

What to Expect in Grief

My emotions may be all over the place. But that is considered
normal.

Sabrina Black

Heal me, LORD. . . .
I am worn out from my groaning.
All night long I flood my bed with weeping and
    drench my couch with tears.

Psalm 6:2, 6

aving an idea of what is normal in grief and what to
expect will help you in the midst of this confusing,
exhausting time. As you read this chapter, you'll
discover thoughts and emotions commonly experienced by
people grieving a death. We want to assure you that what
you're experiencing is normal, yet unique.

Your Grief Is Unique

You've attended funerals. You've comforted grieving friends. You've seen death on TV. Now it's your turn. Having observed grief from a distance, you knew it would be rough. But you didn't think it would be like this. Sandy, whose son died, describes grief this way:

> You go outside and look around and you wonder why the whole world doesn't stop for this period of time. People are still going to amusement parks and eating ice cream cones. Don't they know what horrific thing has gone on? It's like a nightmare.

Adding to the pain is the fact that well-meaning friends do not truly understand what you're going through. But that's okay. Grieving with hope begins, in part, by recognizing that what you're feeling is unique to you.

"No one else really understands the depth of your love and the depth of your feeling for the one who has died," shares Zig Ziglar, motivational speaker whose daughter died. "People can say, 'I know how you feel.' But the reality is no one knows how much you loved the one you lost."

Other people cannot comprehend the specific nature and depth of your pain because the details woven together to form your relationship were unique to that relationship. Sabrina Black, family counselor, explains:

> Even though you may talk to ten parents who have lost a child, ten women who have lost a husband, or ten men who have lost a wife, every situation is different because of our relationships, our backgrounds, the way we process things, the dynamics between the two of us. Our situation is unique to us.

Although your grief experience will not mirror anyone else's, grieving people often struggle with similar thoughts and emotions. Throughout this book, we've compiled the experiences and advice of people who've faced grief and found hope. Finding out what's normal in grief and what to expect will help ease your mind and keep you moving forward through your grief process.

Common Experiences on the Journey of Grief

Depression

One of the most common reactions to the death of a loved one is a deep feeling of sadness. Low energy, fatigue, trouble sleeping, difficulty making decisions, and feelings of hopelessness often accompany the sadness.

"My mother would wonder why I kept the room so dark and why I was lying down so much," shares Kimberly, who lost her grandmother. "That's how I wanted it. I wanted it quiet, I didn't want to eat, and I didn't want to be bothered. I would look at the phone and just watch it ring."

Susan Zonnebelt-Smeenge, a Christian psychologist, said that after her husband's death "it felt like there was nothing left, that my life was over."

During grief, these types of depressed feelings are natural, but how do you know if you should be concerned about the length or severity of these feelings? Talk with your doctor. Talk with your pastor. They can give you wise feedback on how you are navigating the grief process. You could even ask them, "Do you think I'm making enough progress on my grief journey?" Also, spend time with others who know what grief is like. They can encourage you, which can keep you from getting too depressed. But if in your depression you begin to entertain thoughts of suicide, talk with someone who's been trained in suicide prevention right away.

Feeling like You're Losing Your Mind

You likely find it difficult to concentrate and make simple decisions. You lose track of time. You may forget your friends' names, how to get places, and other basic facts. If mental glitches are causing problems at work or home, write down what you need to do and ask others for help in making decisions. Scaling back on how much you're trying to do can be beneficial, as your body may be telling you that you need more time before going full speed again.

H. Norman Wright, grief therapist and trauma specialist, describes some mental capacities that may not function as well during your grief:

> In grief your memory plays tricks on you. There are things you remember, but then you wonder, *Did that really happen?* You may be talking to someone and all of a sudden, *What was I talking about?* When you're in grief, you don't concentrate very well, and the person you lost often dominates your mind.

What's most important is this: do not get frustrated with yourself. Your mind and body are on emotional overload.

Feelings of Denial

You can expect feelings of denial at first—denial that your loved one is truly gone, denial that you can go on without your loved one. Denial helps you portion out your pain to a degree you can handle at that moment. It's natural, and it's helpful. At some point you must move beyond denial, but at the beginning it's to be expected.

Joanne's ten-year-old son died in a car accident. She shares:

> I was in denial in the beginning. I didn't want to leave my house for fear that my son would come home and I would miss him. I also thought if I kept his things around me, kept his pictures next to me, cried over them all the time, that would keep me close to him.

Denial helps by buffering the shock of your loss. But as you might suspect, denial can also become a problem. This happens when you continue to believe your life can go back to the way it was and when you think happiness can be found only in the way things used to be.

Denial is also a problem when you deny that you are hurting or that you need help from others. You may say, "I'm okay; I can handle this on my own—I *am* handling this," when you aren't. Denial then becomes a crutch, and you need to admit how you really feel about your situation and accept help from others.

Physical Problems

Directly or indirectly, grief affects every area of your life. You may experience physical difficulties. Due to your fatigue, lack of energy, and overall stress, you may be more susceptible to colds and viruses. You may have heart palpitations or dizziness. Your stomach can feel queasy. Headaches can result from tension, fatigue, or dehydration.

Be aware of how you feel. Visit a doctor if you don't feel well, as your symptoms may be the result of a problem other than grief. Make conscious daily decisions to do what is right to keep up your physical health. Eat healthy food, drink lots of water, and make a point to get some type of exercise, even if it's just a short walk in the fresh air. Take time to rest, but don't overdo the amount of time you spend in bed.

Relief

If your loved one experienced a long illness before his or her death, you may have feelings of relief—relief that your loved one is no longer suffering, relief that your days aren't overwhelmed with hospitals, feedings, cleaning, assisting, and taking care of your loved one's needs. Be comforted by the fact that relief is never something to be ashamed of; it has nothing to do with your love for the person who died. It's a normal response to an exhausting and difficult situation.

"During Mom's last few months," says Judy Blore, director of an organization that helps the bereaved, "I was begging the Lord to give Mom a ticket home. On the day she died, I was relieved that she was no longer suffering, yet I hated that death came and I couldn't stop it. I was relieved that we didn't have to care for her anymore, and I was relieved for my husband that my life was not controlled by my busyness with something else."

A Tangled Ball of Emotions

Picture a ball of yarn, not neatly rolled but with knotted, overlapping strands and sections tangled together. What a mess to sort through . . . but it *can* be done. Your emotions in grief are like that tangled ball: knotted, jumbled, and confusing.

Before your loved one's death, you had certain ideas of what emotions a grieving person would experience. But until you experienced the death, you did not truly realize the variety of intense, unpredictable emotions intertwined: anguish, anger, loneliness, regret, guilt, apathy, fear, and more. Sometimes your emotions feel so tangled that it's difficult to distinguish what emotions you are feeling. This is a common experience.

> What you're going through is normal. You are experiencing so many different emotions in grief, and you're not used to having to process that many emotions all at once. Your emotions all seem to be coming at a rapid pace, and because they're coming so quickly, you're overwhelmed by them. These things will slow down at some point. It won't be right away. Tomorrow you'll probably still feel like you're losing your mind. Just hold on. It gets better.
>
> Sabrina Black

Accept that your emotions are a tangled ball and that this is to be expected. Sorting through a tangled ball takes patience, perseverance, and deliberation. Winston Smith, counselor, recommends, "Don't edit or censor what you're feeling. Those powerful kinds of feelings are normal, and they won't hurt you. Let the feelings expose the questions of your soul so that you know exactly what you need to be bringing to the Lord and asking for help with."

Spiritual Dryness

While many people turn to the Lord during their grief, others have no desire for prayer, Bible reading, or church. If that's how you feel, tell the Lord. Ask him to give you a desire for these things; they are crucial for your healing even though they may seem difficult to do. Here are some other suggestions to help you:

> Some days I would just get the car keys, go to my church, and ask for a pastor or someone else who would pray with me.
>
> Connie

> Get your Bible out and open it to any place because the Bible says that all Scripture is beneficial. Meditate on the Word of God.
>
> Sabrina Black

> Many bereaved people say, "My prayers are dried up. I don't want to read the Bible. I appear to have lost my faith." And I will say to them, "No, you've not lost your faith at all. You can't pray because frankly you don't know what to say. But nevertheless you can exist in a comfortable silence with the Lord at this point: 'I don't know what to say, but I'm here.'" Then little by little the threads are picked up again.
>
> Rev. Richard Bewes

> To go to church can seem very intimidating, but church is a resource that's going to put you in contact with people who can help you grow. If you can overcome that fear of walking in the door, and then make yourself available to what God

can do through that, you'll see the benefits available to you and you'll find there are a lot of people who feel exactly like you do.

Lois Rabey, author, speaker, and widow

I continued to do the things I knew would keep me close to God, even when I was angry about the deaths, even though sometimes when reading the Bible I would close it and think, *I don't feel better*. Because God was my hope, I still wanted to read, I still wanted to pray, I still went to church. Even though there was an absence of joy, I knew that didn't mean God had left. I knew as time passed God would do the healing. That was the hope I held on to, and he did.

Nancy

Emotional Ambushes

Some books teach that you will pass through and complete certain levels or stages of grief. The reality is you will jump back and forth. You may be well into the grieving process, thinking you're doing fine, when an emotion hits. And it feels as strong as it did those first few weeks. Even several years after a death, intense emotions can be triggered by certain memories, events, smells, and sounds. We call this being ambushed by grief. As Meb says, "Grief is a funny thing. You feel like you're pretty stable, and all of a sudden, you're not."

What has triggered an emotional ambush for you? It may be a song on the radio, a person who resembles your loved one, an item in the grocery store, a letter in the mail addressed to your loved one, a smell, a sound, a news story.

Norm, Jan, and John share their experiences with un-expected emotions:

Eight years after Matthew died, we had a young man working in the yard. I talked to him, and I came inside and was really bothered. I didn't know why.

My wife looked at me, and the tears were coming down her face. She said, "He looks just like Matthew." The coloring of his face, the hairline, the eyes. It brought back that sense of loss once again, and we just held one another and wept.

But on the other side of it, it was a blessing because God had allowed us a peek at what Matthew might have looked like had he lived.

H. Norman Wright

I'm in the grocery store, and I can go down that aisle ten times and not be bothered. Then the eleventh time I see something he loved, and it makes me cry. So I cry a little bit, and that's okay.

Jan

We are never safe from the unguarded moment. When my mother had been dead for about a year, I was at a local coffee shop reading a newspaper. From behind me I heard this click, click, click. It was an elderly person with a walker who was coming in. All of a sudden, I had tears in my eyes. All it took was a sound. My mom had the same kind of walker.

John Trent, president of StrongFamilies

A Word of Encouragement

No matter how long you've been grieving, you will make it through. What you are experiencing right now is a normal part of the grief process. The people who share their insights in this book have been there; they have an understanding of what you are facing. Let the words in this book guide you in knowing what to expect and how to respond as you move forward through this necessary time of grieving.

2

Coping with Grief

People will say, "You've got to be brave. You've got to be strong." When you're grieving, that's not the time to be brave. That's not the time to be strong. You need to be human.

Zig Ziglar

So do not fear, for I am with you;
    do not be dismayed, for I am your God.
I will strengthen you and help you;
    I will uphold you with my righteous right hand.

Isaiah 41:10

Since each person's grief is unique, there's no one way to deal with the pain you'll experience on your journey toward healing. There are, however, many who've gone before you. Some of them spent time talking with us because they wanted to help others. They shared what their grief was like—what worked and what didn't. The following are some simple and practical steps many of them took to deal with the overwhelming nature of grief.

Know That Grief Is an Expression of Love

Daily, we hear about death—the death of movie stars, politicians, athletes, and other influential people. Local news tells us about murders and fatal car accidents. World news tells us about war casualties, epidemics, and deaths caused by natural disasters. Yet, despite the number of deaths we hear about, often we're unmoved. Granted, we may think, *That's awful* or *What a tragedy*. Sometimes we may even make a donation to help.

But your reaction to hearing about a death in the news is nothing like the grief you're experiencing now. Why is that? As Zig Ziglar says, it's because grief is a by-product of love. He says, "Grief is the recognition that you've lost someone you love. It's the price you pay for loving someone, because if there were no love, there'd be no grief."

Grief can be debilitating. It can be something you desperately want to escape. So strong and powerful are the emotions of grief that you may even begin to wonder if something is wrong with you. Understanding that grief is the recognition of your love for the person you lost can help you to be patient with yourself as you grieve.

Do the Next Thing

Grief can cloud your mind, paralyze your body, and make simple tasks difficult. Edward Welch, counselor, shares a practical piece of advice: do the next thing.

> It sounds like fairly shallow counsel, granted. But grief and suffering can feel like such a weight that they can immobilize you. It can feel like once you're immobilized, you will never

start again. Oftentimes people in bereavement will say, "Okay, I need to do the next thing." What is the next thing? It can be very ordinary. It could be getting a glass of water; it could be brushing your teeth; it could be taking a shower; it could be making a phone call; it could be vacuuming; it could be going to work.

As you wake to each new day, say out loud what you need to do next. Tell yourself to get out of bed, take a shower, and make yourself breakfast. Do the next thing one step, one moment, at a time.

Another idea is to keep a small notebook, handheld computer, notepad, or recording device handy. Record what you need to do each day as the tasks come to mind, even the simplest tasks. Grief makes it difficult to concentrate and to remember, so this activity will help you stay on track.

Patricia, who experienced the deaths of two of her children, her husband, and her father, shares a Bible verse that kept her moving forward each day: "My verse is 'I can do all things through Christ who strengthens me' (Phil. 4:13). That's what got me out of bed every day, that's what kept me going minute by minute." You too can embrace this Bible verse—this promise from God—for yourself. He will provide the strength you need daily to accomplish each task as it comes.

Postpone Big Decisions

What decisions are you facing as a result of the death? Selling the house? Changing jobs? Relocating? Unless you *must* make the decision now, postpone the decision for at least a year.

H. Norman Wright explains:

> Sometimes when you're in grief, you don't make the best decisions. They could be out of impulse. In doing that, you could generate another major loss in your life. For instance, you may say, "I just can't live in this house anymore. I'm

going to sell it." After you sell it, you realize you were there for thirty years, and you have so many memories that are there, and you've taken away the opportunity to process those memories of your loved one who has died because you're no longer in that home.

Talk with others about decisions you are facing. Seek people who give wise, expert, biblically based counsel. Grief author Lorraine Peterson says, "Seek a person who is able to give you competent advice, a person who is a strong and committed Christian but also knowledgeable in the area. For example, if you have to make a real estate decision, talk to someone who can help you in that area. If it's a business decision, find someone who knows about business. Ask God to put the right people in your path who can help you make those decisions."

Once you've received wise counsel, prayerfully weigh the pros and cons of your options. As you decide, remember that the way you feel now may not be how you will always feel. Take time to pray about your decision, being sure to look to God's Word for guidance instead of telling God what you're going to do.

You may think you are capable of making a good decision right now, but Robert DeVries, seminary professor, who experienced his wife's death, says, "We don't always think straight. You may think you are thinking straight, but as a matter of fact, your mind is clouded with all the emotions and the experiences that are going on. I know that on my own grief journey it took me quite a while to make what I thought were responsible decisions."

Lean into Your Grief

Many people try to push down their emotions and hurt, stuffing the pain and anguish inside in order to get through the day. This doesn't work. In fact, it makes grief last longer.

Sandy, whose son died from cancer, was living what she describes as a nightmare. Drained and despairing, she sought advice from a friend who had also lost a son.

"Karen," I said, "How do you do this?"

She said, "I'm going to tell you something that sounds kind of cold. The best thing to do is to lean into it. Just take it like waves of an ocean. Don't try to run from it. Don't try to numb it. Don't try to pretend it isn't so. It's part of your life, so feel everything. Smell everything. Be in all the moments."

Looking back maybe a year or so down the road, I could say that was some of the best counsel I was given. Simply to lean into the grief, to embrace it. You don't have to like it. That's not what that means. It means you let it take you where it will, and you will go to places in your soul you've never been.

We understand how difficult it is to let yourself mourn, cry, and express your emotions. But fully experiencing grief is one of the most important things to do to experience comfort and healing. Consciously acknowledge and feel each of your feelings. Accept that this is the norm right now. You won't always feel this way, but for now, find a place, time, and way to let your emotions out.

Move toward God

During grief, people move either away from God or toward him. But understand that when you move away from him, you hinder yourself from receiving the help he offers. Listen to the help God wants to give to those who are weary and weak:

> Do you not know?
>   Have you not heard? . . .
> He gives strength to the weary
>   and increases the power of the weak.

Even youths grow tired and weary,
    and young men stumble and fall;
but those who hope in the LORD
    will renew their strength.
They will soar on wings like eagles;
    they will run and not grow weary,
    they will walk and not be faint. (Isa. 40:28–31)

Take this time to develop your relationship with God. Get to know his character. Learn about his promises. Try to see things from his eternal perspective, for God has already begun a plan to put an end to all suffering and pain. And the plan will ultimately produce a world in which "he will wipe every tear from their eyes. There will be no more death or mourning or crying or pain, for the old order of things has passed away" (Rev. 21:4).

As you learn about God, don't forget to talk to him. The Bible says to "cast all your anxiety on him because he cares for you" (1 Peter 5:7). That means he can handle anything that's on your mind—your worries, fears, doubts, and anger.

Elisabeth Elliot's first husband was murdered. Several years later she remarried, and her second husband died from cancer. She talks about what it means to offer her grief to God and the benefits of doing so:

> As I was lying in bed one night before Addison (my second husband) died, I was so helpless and feeling so afraid of the future. I was thinking, "I can't stand one more day of this." It was as if the Lord told me then, "Offer up your pain." I felt like saying to the Lord, "I offer you my pain, Lord, but what is the good of that? What use can you make of it?" It was as though the Lord was smiling at me lovingly and saying, "That's not your problem. I will take care of that."
>
> So after the deaths of my two husbands, I did that. Daily, whenever the dagger would stab my heart, which we all know it does at unexpected moments, I would offer it up. If I was in a place by myself, I would lift up my hands and say, "Lord,

here's my pain. I give it to you. Now transform it for the good of others."

I had heard a sermon when I was in Wheaton College, and I have never forgotten one phrase. A missionary woman said, "If your life is broken when given to Jesus, it may be because the pieces will feed a multitude."

Commit to a Grief Recovery Group

A grief recovery support group is a place where other people know the depth and intensity of your pain, and they know how difficult it is to deal with friends, co-workers, and even family members who do not understand. At a Bible-based grief recovery group, you will have the opportunity to learn more about the grief process and how it is affecting you. You'll learn how to take steps forward and grieve in a way that is healthy.

Although your grief is unique, you will meet people who have an idea of what you are feeling. You'll find that others really do relate to how you are feeling. More importantly, you'll realize how much God relates to your feelings and why he is the best comforter for you.

When attending a group, be sure to take an active role in your healing. Make a commitment to learn. Take notes. Do the homework. When you're ready, participate in the discussions. These steps help tremendously. (GriefShare® support groups are located across the US, Canada, and in other countries. Visit www.griefshare.org or call 800-395-5755 to find a group near you.)

A Word of Encouragement

You are grieving because you are a person who has loved another. That is the reason for the feelings you are having today. Since your grief response is a response of love, facing, expressing, and coping with your emotions can be seen as an expression of honor toward, and remembrance of, your relationship.

If you are confused about the relationship you had with the person you lost and are hesitant to call it a loving relationship, that's okay too. You're not alone in feeling this way, and we will talk more in later chapters about how to cope with those confusing emotions.

3

Will This Pain Ever End?

This grief is temporary. In the beginning, it feels like it's going
to last forever. Oh, how it feels like it's going to last forever.

Joanne

How long must I wrestle with my thoughts
and day after day have sorrow in my heart?

Psalm 13:2

This chapter discusses how to move through your pain
and the importance of not rushing the grieving process.
We recommend jotting down your thoughts in a print
or electronic journal as you consider the insights, questions,
and ideas in this chapter.

Why Grief Takes So Long

A common cry of people in grief is, "It feels like my grief
will never end. I will be in this dark pit forever. Will my pain

go away? Will this sadness engulf me forever?" Rest assured, your pain will go away, but not completely. That doesn't mean you'll never smile again, though. As you move through this book, you'll discover that peace and pain can coexist. You'll find you can function in much the same way you did before you lost your loved one and still honor your loved one's memory.

While your pain will never completely disappear, it won't always hurt as much as it does now. The length and severity of your pain depends on factors such as

- whom you lost
- the dynamics of that relationship
- how close you were to that person
- the manner of death
- the age of the person who died

It also depends on

- your willingness to choose to move forward in healthy grieving
- how much effort you put into healthy grieving
- the degree to which you allow God to comfort you and to direct your daily life

With the death of a loved one, you have lost more than just a person. You have lost everything that ties in with that person, every role that person played in your life, every dream you had that included that person. You may grieve the loss of conversations, opinions, advice, laughter, companionship, dreams, and plans, not to mention the more concrete losses of someone to do the bills, cook, snuggle with, sit with in church and at dinner, and assist with housework and other household responsibilities. To help you take the important step of identifying and grieving each of your losses, make a list of everything you have lost connected with your loved one.

One by one, face the items on your list by first praying for God's comfort and guidance in helping you grieve that loss.

You will also find that past losses intensify current losses. Past losses need to be acknowledged, accepted, and honestly grieved over too. You might be thinking, *I don't want to go there. I don't want to open that door.* But you need to. The Bible says that by grieving these losses, you will receive the comfort God has for you: "Blessed are those who mourn, for they will be comforted" (Matt. 5:4). Honest, thorough grieving leads to comfort and healing.

Winston Smith recommends thinking back to your past and asking yourself:

- How many ways have I experienced loss?
- Have I grieved those past losses? How did I express my grief?
- How did I turn to the Lord or not turn to the Lord?
- How do I see God's faithfulness so that when I look to my future I can have hope?

Develop a New Normal

Developing a new normal is part of how you will move through your pain and begin to see it diminish. Before your loved one's death, the daily patterns and interactions in your life were what you would have called normal. Today you may find yourself wishing that life would go back to normal. Unfortunately, you can never go back to, or even re-create, your past. It's gone. Instead, you must seek to establish a new normal in your life. Your new normal is one in which your loved one is no longer with you and your daily patterns have changed. But a new normal can be good, and it will help you through your pain.

You can choose what you want your new normal to look like. It will be a slow process, but it will have positive results.

Consider these points as you daily seek to establish a new normal. (It can be helpful to write down answers to these questions as you try to sort through your thoughts.)

1. Which parts of your daily schedule must you remain committed to (job, family members, other responsibilities)? How have these commitments changed since the death?
2. Regarding the commitments that have changed, which changes would you prefer to keep, which changes are not helping you, and what could you do to make those situations better? In other words, what would be a better normal in terms of your daily experience at work, your interactions with family members, and how you fulfill your other responsibilities?
3. What daily rituals, family traditions and interactions, and leisure activities have changed, or will change, as a result of the death?
4. Consider which of these you'd like to continue to incorporate into your life. Consider which would be better as precious memories, and begin to incorporate new rituals, traditions, and activities that better suit your new situation.

One of the trickiest aspects of creating a new normal is doing so without guilt. Why might you feel guilt? As you decide what traditions and activities you want in your new normal, you'll realize that you probably did a lot of things (e.g., watching sports, listening to certain types of music, eating at certain restaurants) because your loved one enjoyed them. Moving forward, you may feel as if you are betraying your loved one by deciding not to do those things. Rest assured, although you may feel uncomfortable leaving those things behind, those decisions don't mean you love the person you lost any less.

Developing your new normal is a key part of your journey of grief. But it's not without its challenges. We'll share more about how to do it and what it will look like for you in chapter 6.

Don't Let People Rush You Past the Pain

Because most people truly don't understand the depth of your grief, they may make comments that cause you to feel the need to hurry up and get past your grief and pain. Do not let people rush you. Going the length of your journey—with no shortcuts or detours—is crucial to your healing. This is why Sabrina Black says it's important for you to "feel what you feel and allow the Lord to comfort you":

> Our society says, "You should be over that. That was two weeks ago; that was two months ago." The tendency is to put on a mask and pretend you're okay. But you have to be honest with people and let them know this is not helping. You need to say, "This is what I feel. I need to experience this. I'm planning to get to the other side of it, but I'm not there yet."

Most people you interact with have never walked the path you are on, and while they may care deeply, it is difficult for them because they can't fix you. They don't have the answers, and they can't understand how you are feeling. They think they are helping you when they encourage you to get on with your life.

Don't Try to Rush Yourself

In your case, perhaps other people are not rushing you but rather *you* are the one trying to get over your pain as quickly as possible. Yes, your pain will fade, but only when you face and work through the tough days of grief.

Robert DeVries's wife of twenty-eight years died of cancer. He shares:

> One of the first responses I had after Char died was to say, "I've got to get through this as fast as I can." That is probably a typical male response. "I'm going to fix it. I've got to be a problem solver."

Over time, I began to realize there was no way I could ever begin to fix this. As a matter of fact, I did a lot of things I would consider now to be the wrong way of handling it. I started to remodel the kitchen. That took me about nine months. Char had always wanted the kitchen remodeled, and it was only after I finished it that emotionally I realized she wasn't even there to experience it.

That was probably one of the first times I began to accept the fact that I couldn't hurry through this grief or divert myself from it. I had to take time to focus on the grief, to stop working on the kitchen, to stop throwing myself into my job, and to sit and really work at my grief.

A good friend of mine on the golf course finally reminded me of something very simple that I knew in my head but in my heart I didn't. He said, "Look, Bob, it took you twenty-eight years to grow together. Don't expect to heal overnight." So that's the difficult part: to be patient while you're going through that grieving process because it's going to take a long time to heal.

A Word of Encouragement

There is hope. "Scripture talks about how the Lord will turn your mourning into dancing, so expect that at some point you will dance again," says Sabrina Black. "You will rejoice again, but it is going to take some time to get there."

Again, things will get better. You will begin to experience peace, joy, and healing as you continue to learn and put into practice how to grieve in a healthy manner.

4

Healthy Ways to Relieve Your Pain

Comfort is interesting because, like the experience of grief, the experience of comfort is not the same in everybody.

Paul Tripp, pastor and counselor

Cast all your anxiety on him because he cares for you.

1 Peter 5:7

To heal from grief, it's important to know what brings you comfort, because what brings other people comfort may not help you at all. This chapter suggests practices that may bring comfort to you or may spark an idea of something else you might do to find comfort.

Everyone Finds Comfort in Different Ways

Just as you grieve differently than other people, you also experience comfort in your own way. What comforts someone else may not comfort you, and vice versa. "Somebody else's road map, somebody else's style, and somebody else's choices may not be the best or most useful things for you," says Judy Blore.

For example, your friend may be strengthened by the presence of others; she welcomes a house full of guests. You, on the other hand, may prefer to be alone or cared for by an individual, not a mob. In this case, what brings your friend comfort doesn't help you heal at all. It actually disturbs you. This is why discovering and then making time to do what comforts you are a big part of your grief journey. Such actions allow you to make progress in your healing.

How do you figure out what comforts you? Paul Tripp suggests that you ask yourself, *What are the things in the last couple of weeks that I found to be most comforting?* and then "go there and grab hold of them. Find those things, and thank God he's provided those resources for you." Think back over the last week or two. What healthy experiences brought you some comfort, even if only for a short moment? Those moments may provide clues as to where you can find the lasting, healing comfort God has in store for you.

The rest of this chapter offers a few suggestions on how you might find comfort. As you look them over, keep in mind that you may be surprised at what comforts you. As you try to discover what helps, it's important that you (1) recognize your need for comfort, (2) are open to receiving and accepting comfort, and (3) understand you may need to take steps to find healthy practices that work for you.

Healthy Ways to Find Comfort

Listen to Music

You may struggle with despairing thoughts, false guilt, and negative images. Listening to music can be an effective way of finding comfort. Consider carrying headphones and a portable music player, bringing a CD to put in your computer at work, or tuning your radio to a Christian station. Good Christian songs speak words of truth and can help you replace negative thoughts such as *I can't go on* with positive thoughts such as *This will be difficult, but with God's help I can make it.*

> We had some CDs with songs that were all Scripture and words of comfort, and I would sit sometimes for two or three hours and close my eyes and listen because I was too weary to read the Bible. I would feel like my cup was being refilled.
>
> Ann

> I urge people, just before they go to bed at night, to put on good, soft, sweet gospel music, listening to God's promises, God's grace, God's hope, and God's redemption.
>
> Zig Ziglar

Spend Time Outdoors

Being outside is good for you. Not only are there physical benefits from the exercise and fresh air, but there are mental and spiritual benefits too. Spending time in nature reminds us of the beauty and intricacies of God's creation. Just as many writers in the Bible have discovered, looking at the trees, the sky, and the sun takes your mind off negative thoughts and inspires worship of the Creator: "The heavens proclaim the glory of God," declares the psalmist. "The skies display his craftsmanship. Day after day they continue to speak; night after night they make him known" (Ps. 19:1–2 NLT).

Consider taking time for one of the following outdoor activities:

- take a walk and just breathe in the fresh air and notice the sun, the grass, the water, the colors
- work in the yard, building, repairing, cleaning
- go to the beach and watch the waves roll in

- bring a child to a park or play catch or jump rope
- ride a bike, cross-country ski, play tennis or basketball
- walk a dog
- hike a mountain trail
- tend a garden for yourself or someone else
- a different outdoor activity of your choice

Get a Pet

Pets are wonderful listeners and comforters. If a larger pet is not possible for you, visit a pet store and consider a smaller one. You might be surprised at all the choices.

My daughter worked near a pet store, and she kept after me about going to look at this miniature German schnauzer, and I kept saying, "No, not interested." Finally, one day she said, "Dad, we've got the time; let's just look at that schnauzer." So I said, "Okay, but I'm just looking." I came home with two schnauzers, and they have been really good for me. They've been a lot of work, but we're good friends now, and they've helped me through the loneliness. They give me something other than pictures and things to talk to. I tell them about my wife.

Bruce

Write in a Journal

Writing down thoughts and feelings is an effective way to release your emotions and feel a sense of comfort. Get a notebook or journal, or pull out your laptop. Not sure what to write? Write down what happened today. How did you feel when that happened? What was the best part of your day? What was the worst part of your day?

Use your journal to list emotions you are feeling and thoughts that are spinning around in your mind. Write a letter to your deceased loved one. Write songs, write Scripture verses, write poems to honor your loved one. Write prayers to God. Carry your journal with you so you can write in it as new situations or feelings occur.

Your journal does not have to be neat. It doesn't have to contain proper grammar and correct spelling. Your journal is there as a healing tool, for your eyes only. It provides the opportunity to face and deal with tough situations; it gives you a place to release pent-up emotions.

Look at or Create Memorabilia

Looking through a photo album can bring a flood of healing tears and happy memories. Consider making a collage with photos and mementos of times spent with your loved one. Fill the blank spaces in your collage with words that describe your loved one and phrases or sayings that remind you of him or her.

A scrapbook is another idea. What about a painting, drawing, sculpture, ornament, or wood craft of something that reminds you of your loved one? You could also create items to give to family members as gifts of remembrance.

Look at Your Sympathy Cards or Funeral Video

Another way to relieve your pain is to look at the cards you received when your loved one died. When you received those cards, you likely were numb, and you may not remember who sent them or what they said. Seeing the cards now will remind you of people who care, and some cards may contain meaningful words about your loved one.

If you have one, you may want to watch the video of the funeral. While initially this may cause you more pain, you may later find comfort in it. Leaning into your emotions helps you to work through grief and to heal.

It's tough to want to face the pain, but only by facing pain do people work their way through grief. If we are afraid of doing something, it really has more power over us than we have over it. So being able to put your hand on the burner and face some of those hard things could end up being a blessing for grieving people, where they may later say, "I'm glad I did that; that was so helpful."

Susan Zonnebelt-Smeenge

Serve Others

Stepping outside yourself to help other people is a practice that has proven successful in relieving personal pain. Because of the emotional overload that accompanies grief, you are understandably focused on yourself. Even though you might not be at a place yet where you can turn your focus away from yourself, be aware that at some point you'll need to.

The type of help you provide for others will be uniquely suited to you, and it should be something that brings you comfort and not stress. Whom can you help? What help can you provide? Ask God these questions, then continue to ask him throughout the week as you look at people around you with a greater awareness. Remember that while your struggles may seem so much worse to you than those of your co-worker who is struggling with a marriage, your elderly neighbor who does not get around very well, your friend who is a single parent, or your relative who has lost a job, people around you are hurting in different ways, and they could use your help.

You might choose to wait until your strength returns before helping someone else, but strength often returns *as* you serve others, so give it a try.

"The week after Hope died," shares Christian author Nancy Guthrie, "I read a book by a man who lost a child. He wrote that serving others was the only thing that helped him overcome his pain. Honestly, I didn't believe it would make a difference, but I was desperate for something to relieve my pain. I decided to give it a try.

"My friend Angela, a mother of three who had lost her husband about a year earlier, had just moved to my neighborhood. David and I could see that her house was in need of yard work. So we loaded up our lawn tools, went over to her house, and began to work. I found that as I served someone else, it lessened my pain."

> Some of God's best ministers are ordinary folks who have gotten their PhD in the school of suffering and now are eminently qualified to help other people.
>
> Pray for eyes that are open to see the hurts and pains of people around you. Pray that he will show you the people you can help.
>
> Pastor Ray Pritchard

Read the Psalms

When the writer of Psalm 88 cries out to God about his feelings of weakness, lowness, heaviness, and despair and then finally declares, "The darkness is my closest friend," you can probably relate. Reading the Psalms can be a great source of comfort because the psalmists are completely real and honest with God about their feelings. You may find they sometimes express what you're feeling better than you can!

> I have found Psalm 69 to be helpful. It talks about how the water is coming up over your head and you feel like you're drowning. That's what it's like to be in the depths of grief.
>
> As you read the psalm, it pulls you out of that and allows you to understand how God is a God of love and refuge who will rescue you. It brings you out of that despair into who God is, and it leaves you knowing God is there for you. Most psalms draw you from a place where maybe you've put yourself to a place where you can see God and know who he is.
>
> Kristi

Go to God

When you are in the process of grieving, you may feel like you are in the midst of an emotional storm. And just like in a crashing hurricane, if you have a strong tower or fortress to go to and a solid rock to place your feet on, you will be able to survive.

The Bible refers to God as a fortress. "He is my rock and my salvation; he is my fortress, I will never be shaken" (Ps. 62:2). God is a rock and a secure fortress because he never changes. No matter how bleak your situation has become, his promises of love, support, and comfort remain true. This is why we can cling to him in the midst of confusion. His love and concern for us are the same yesterday, today, and forever. So how do you experience God as a rock or a fortress? These individuals share their insights:

> I remind myself regularly that he will never leave us or forsake us. The world can drag you down if you let it. It's good to remember God's promises.
>
> Jeff

> Sometimes the pain of grief blinds us to the fact that God is always with us; we hurt so much we can't imagine anything but our own pain. In those times we need a Christian friend to remind us that what the Bible says is true and that truth is not dependent on feelings.
>
> Connie

> Stop, relax, and spend more time talking to God, praying, and saying, "Help me get through this." Try not to put pressure on yourself; know that God is going to get you through.
>
> Susan

Are You Seeking Comfort in Ways That Are Unhealthy?

If you aren't making choices to find comfort in ways that are healthy, are you making potentially harmful choices that will prolong and intensify your grief? It's good to seek comfort from your pain, but it's unhealthy to numb it. Numbing your pain can be done in a variety of ways—some of which may surprise you.

Eating too much, shopping for things you don't need, and overworking are popular choices. Sleeping, watching television, keeping busy, surfing the internet, and taking prescription medications are also unhealthy practices when you do them to forget your pain. Pornography, affairs, unhealthy sexual relations, illicit drugs, and alcohol will ultimately harm you and those around you and will increase the pain you're already experiencing.

Not one of these practices actually brings comfort. They may temporarily dull the pain, but they don't do a thing to get rid of it. It is better to face the pain and to seek to endure it with God's help.

> Here's what the desire to numb says: "I'm alone; no one understands; I don't have the capacity to go through this, so somehow I've got to escape." These are all lies.
>
> The minute I move toward numbing my pain, I am denying the most significant reality of my existence: I'm not in this moment by myself. There is a God who has committed himself to being with me. He promises he will never turn his back on me in my moment of need.
>
> Paul Tripp

If you are struggling with finding healthy ways to relieve the pain and receive comfort, consider attending a Christ-centered grief support group. You will learn practical ideas on living with grief and how to work through your grief. You will be able to relax and spend time with people who truly have an idea of what you're feeling and facing each day. Taking the step of attending a group can be scary, but once you get there, you may find it was the best step you've taken yet. (GriefShare® groups meet across the nation, Canada, and around the world. To find the groups nearest you, visit www.griefshare.org or call 800-395-5755 for caring, personal assistance.)

A Word of Encouragement

God has created you to receive comfort in your own way. Some people will experience comfort in large doses, and others experience it one brief moment at a time. Keep your eyes open for things in daily life that you find comforting, and be sure to thank God when you experience comfort, because he alone is the source of comfort (2 Cor. 1:3).

5

Feeling Alone

I know he hasn't forsaken me, but this is a really lonely place to be.

Molly

He will never leave you nor forsake you. Do not be afraid.

Deuteronomy 31:8

Loneliness is a difficult emotion for people grieving a loved one's death. It's an experience that cannot be fully understood by a person who has never been there. This chapter will help you pinpoint why you're struggling with loneliness, and it will guide you on ways to get through the loneliest times.

Reasons You May Struggle with Loneliness

You Believe Lies Based on Your Feelings

Sometimes your feelings are your worst enemy because what you feel is not an accurate gauge of what is true. For instance, you may feel like people don't care about you or your struggles, when in actuality they don't know how to express their care. You may feel that a co-worker is upset with you, when the truth is he is worrying about how he'll pay his mortgage and isn't even thinking about you.

Your feelings, when taken at face value, can also trick you into thinking God has abandoned you. *I feel so alone. I feel like no one cares about me. I feel I can't make it another day. I feel like I'll never be able to smile again.* These are lies based on your feelings instead of God's Word. If you continue to think that way, you'll prolong your grief.

The truth is that God is always by your side; he is always faithful to help you and provide for you. You will make it another day, another week, another month, and you will make it through your grief—one step at a time.

Even if you don't feel God is near, counter that lie with statements of truth. Remind yourself of the blessings you still have. Thank God for them in prayer.

Reading God's Word is a great way to remind yourself of God's promises and goodness to you. Print biblical truths on small pieces of paper you can read throughout the day:

He will never leave you nor forsake you. (Deut. 31:8)

My Presence will go with you, and I will give you rest. (Exod. 33:14)

> God is our refuge and strength,
> an ever-present help in trouble. (Ps. 46:1)

> When you go through deep waters,
> I will be with you.
> When you go through rivers of difficulty,
> you will not drown.
> When you walk through the fire of oppression,
> you will not be burned up;
> the flames will not consume you. (Isa. 43:2 NLT)

Psychology professor Siang-Yang Tan recommends turning God's Words into prayers of thanksgiving, which will affect your feelings. "Make God's Word into a prayer and allow the Lord to speak his Word to you. Then you'll begin to think in a more balanced way, in a more biblical way that has more meaning now, more hope."

You've Isolated Yourself from People

> People would call me, and I wouldn't return the phone calls. I didn't want to talk to anybody because I felt like nobody understood what I was feeling. I kept thinking, *If I can get by myself, then I can get this thing together. I don't need any help. I just need to be by myself.* But you can't do it by yourself. There's no way.
>
> Doreen

Isolating yourself from other people can seem an easy choice when you're deep in grief, but too much isolation will intensify your pain. By giving in to the desire to constantly be alone, you are putting yourself in a position where you cannot easily receive help and healing from others. People will eventually stop calling and stop trying to help. This might be what you currently desire, but it will ultimately harm you. Make decisions today that will keep you moving forward and not cause you to get stuck in your suffering. When the day comes that you realize you need other people, you don't want to look around and realize no one is there because you drove off everyone. You need to be open to accepting help from friends, relatives, the church, and a grief support group.

Betty shares how she benefited from asking for help:

> I was a very independent person. I never asked for help. When my husband was sick, I probably could have used help, and I was bound and determined we were going to do it on our own.
>
> One time a friend was very insistent, and I jokingly said I needed someone to take out my trash. He then came faithfully

every Tuesday night and took my trash to the end of the driveway.

I learned from that experience that people really do want to help. They need to do something. This isn't about me anymore. It's not me begging for help, asking for help. It's more about allowing people to help who feel the need to do something but don't know what to do. If you give them something tangible to do, it's as much for them as it is helping you.

I would never have dreamed of asking somebody to take out my trash, but this friend wanted to do something and that's what he came and did. You need to bite the bullet and do it.

Choosing to cut yourself off from other people is not the answer to your hurt and pain. Proverbs 18:1 speaks about the danger of this choice: "A man who isolates himself seeks his own desire; he rages against all wise judgment" (NKJV). If you've already started falling into a pattern of isolation, start spending time with others with whom you can share your grief.

You Haven't Admitted Your Weakness

Admitting your weakness is key to experiencing God's help. It's why the apostle Paul said, "I will boast all the more gladly about my weaknesses, so that Christ's power may rest on me" (2 Cor. 12:9). God helps those who admit their weakness. So Paul's response to being weakened was to boast about it. Think about that. Boasting about weaknesses is counter to what most people do when they are weakened by grief. We want others to know we're strong, doing well, and holding it together, so we resist letting people know how much we're hurting for fear they will think less of us. But in light of Paul's response to weakness, it's easy to see why that posturing is unwise. Why? Paul realized that when he boasted about his weakness, God lavished his power on him. If you want God to help you, you must admit you need help.

45

This may sting a bit, but you need to hear this sobering truth: when we don't admit our need for help, we're being prideful. What's worse is that God says he resists helping those who are proud. "That is why Scripture says: 'God opposes the proud but shows favor to the humble'" (James 4:6). God delights in helping the weak.

Could it be that God seems distant to you because you're not admitting to him and others your need for help? Give it some thought.

How to Get through the Lonely Times

Find a Balance between Time Alone and Time with Others

Spending time with other people is crucial for your healing. This does not mean, however, that you constantly surround yourself with people or that you move from one social activity to the next to avoid being alone. Robert DeVries says it's important for "people who have experienced a loss to make certain that they balance being with people and having some private moments." This means you'll need to spend time alone working through your grief, perhaps journaling, praying, and reflecting. But it's just as important to find the right people to spend time with—those who will walk alongside you on your grief journey, who will support and encourage you to move forward but will not push. The right people will listen to you and not interrupt. They will allow you to express your emotions. They will pray for you and with you and help you draw closer to God.

> After a significant loss it's not necessarily the quantity of people who are around you that's important but the quality or the kind of support they're going to give. People who've experienced a significant loss need to be able to discern who those people are. Find people who will listen to you tell the

story over and over again, who are willing to ask probing questions, who aren't going to try to give you advice or fix things for you but are willing simply to let you lament and express your feelings—people who will allow you to be yourself in the midst of your grief.

Robert DeVries

Who are these people in my life? you may wonder. Prayerfully consider and ask God which people he has provided for you in this difficult time. Think of family members, church family, friends, neighbors, and support group friends. Do you have children? If so, it is important for them to have a support network that includes wise, caring adults other than yourself. It's also vital for them to see you seeking help from friends and sharing your burden with others. They will learn that it's okay to ask for help and that they don't need to keep their thoughts and feelings inside.

Sharing your grief with others is a way to help you sort through and process the emotions you are feeling. You will also receive help in making wise decisions. Sharing your grief gives you someone to talk with other than yourself, and it keeps Satan from trying to slip even more negative thoughts into your mind.

If you have lost a spouse, share the details of your grief with people of the same sex as you. While you may not be considering a new relationship, the person you are opening up to may be doing just that. Sharing emotions can create an intimacy you're not ready for.

Understand That Relationships with Friends Will Change

One thing you may have noticed since the loss of your loved one is that some of your past relationships have changed. While some friendships have grown stronger, others have grown more distant. For instance, if you've lost a child, you may experience changes in friendships with other parents who have a child the same age as your child was.

Susan Zonnebelt-Smeenge and Lois Rabey share their personal experiences and insights to help you understand why your relationships may change. Understanding this can help you put some feelings of loneliness into perspective.

> I had a friend who was upset because I didn't have time to do the things I used to do with her before my husband's death. We used to play tennis a lot together, and I didn't have time for that. She felt like I didn't have time for her anymore, and the friendship went by the wayside.
>
> It's important for a person in grief to know that some people won't understand and won't be agreeable to the way your life is right now. You have to be able to say to your real friends, "I'd love to be able to do this, but I can't. It doesn't mean I don't care about you or want to be with you, but my life is different now and so I have to handle some things differently." You have to put some limitations on yourself. That may cost some friendships, but if it does, those folks have some growing to do too.
>
> Lois Rabey

> After my husband, Rick, died, my parents saw my pain, and in their love, they wanted to be there to help. I found myself getting multitudes of invitations to spend time with them; they probably would have been happy if I had moved back home. I realized that wasn't the healthiest thing for me. I had to figure out how to face the pain of loneliness in living in a house by myself.
>
> Susan Zonnebelt-Smeenge

Susan also says that widowed people should understand that friendships change for a number of reasons: (1) friends sometimes still see your deceased spouse when they see you and that's painful; (2) there's the fear that "it happened to my friend, so it could also happen to us as a couple"; and

(3) when a person becomes single, sometimes that is perceived as a threat to a coupled relationship. Understanding the effect your loss has on your coupled friends can help you be more sympathetic to them.

The changes you experience in your relationships are not necessarily bad—they are just changes. Relationships constantly fluctuate throughout different seasons of life. Think about the relationships you have that are somehow different now. It's good to recognize and grieve the relationship as it was, but it's also time to embrace and be open to a new kind of relationship either with old friends or with new. Relationships are necessary for your healing.

Maintain Relationships with Old Friends

Keep up friendships with people who knew both you and your loved one. They can listen to you tell stories and then share their own stories. They can help you make decisions because they are more aware of the details surrounding your situation. They know your likes and dislikes. They know your strengths and weaknesses. They know your family. These friends have been a source of help and comfort in the past, and you would like that to continue into the future.

If you are concerned that a friend is avoiding you because he or she does not know how to act around you right now, talk to this person. Let him or her know that you miss the closeness you once had. Some friends may be under the impression that *you* are the one who does not want to continue the friendship. If this is a friendship you want to have, then Susan Zonnebelt-Smeenge advises you to "get up the courage to find the time to meet with that person and talk about it, saying, 'I find that you're somewhat distant to me right now, and I'm wondering if there's some reason for that. What's actually going on? Is there something I'm doing to push you away?'"

After reading this, you may think to yourself, *Wait a minute. I'm the one who's grieving here. I have enough on my mind. I don't want to initiate conversations about renewing friendships. That should be the job of my friends.* Unfortunately, in our culture, most people do not know how to handle a grieving friend. So avoiding you is the easiest answer. The result? You, unfortunately, will often need to be the one who takes the first step to maintain relationships with friends.

> After your loved one died, some of those friendships you thought were solid and good may not be as available to you. And people you didn't expect to have a close relationship with may have come to the fore and surprised you. It's important to recognize that some friendships will be stronger, some will end, and new relationships will come.
>
> Susan Zonnebelt-Smeenge

Make New Friends

Although old friends are precious, Robert DeVries recommends that you look for opportunities to meet people who did not know your loved one. When they interact with you, they will not have to wrestle with their own grief. As a result, they can put their focus on helping and supporting you.

You might wonder, *Where do I find new friends? How do I start up these friendships?* Remember this: other people need friends too. Lorraine Peterson offers helpful suggestions:

1. Maybe this is the first time you ever had to go to church alone and sit alone. Look around. Who else is sitting alone? Sit down and start a conversation. Invite that person out to a restaurant after church.
2. Some of your best friends can be people older than you. People in a retirement or nursing home love company. You'll find some of them to be the most faithful friends you could ever have.

3. A grief support group is a good place to find new friends because the people who attend these groups understand the overwhelming, confusing, seemingly never-ending emotions you are facing. You can always be yourself in this situation.

4. The easiest way to connect with people is to join a ministry where you're helping other people, such as volunteering at a crisis pregnancy center, serving meals at a mission, sorting clothes at a clothing center, or assisting at a shelter. When you work in that kind of situation, your co-workers automatically become your friends.

5. Children make good friends too. If you don't typically come into contact with children, consider volunteering at your local library, helping at a local school or children's hospital, or volunteering in your church's children's ministry. Children are wonderful friends, and they can help you feel better.

Ask God for wisdom in building new relationships. "Maybe before your loved one died, social life was just a given," says Lorraine. "You had your circle of friends, you did all these things together, and all of a sudden you don't fit anymore. Ask God, 'Now whom should I reach out to? Who's a person I should have as my friend?'"

A Word of Encouragement

Jesus is a friend who knows firsthand how you feel. The Bible says he faced suffering as deep as yours. He faced rejection, hunger, torture, loss, and death. He experienced all the emotions you are going through. Bring the pain of your loneliness to Jesus, who truly knows how you feel, where you are in your suffering, and how to bring you comfort: "For you saw my affliction and knew the anguish of my soul" (Ps. 31:7).

6

Adjusting to Your
New Reality

What used to be normal is no longer, and denial does not
get us anywhere good.

Laura Petherbridge, author and speaker

Though the fig tree does not bud . . .
   and the fields produce no food,
though there are no sheep in the pen
   and no cattle in the stalls,
yet I will rejoice in the LORD,
   I will be joyful in God my Savior.

Habakkuk 3:17–18

Trying to make decisions and adjust to daily life without
your loved one can leave you worn-out and confused.
This chapter provides practical steps on how to create
a new normal for your life.

Death did more than end your relationship with your loved one; it also ended life as you knew it. Now, questions abound. Who am I? How will I spend my time? How will I adjust to my new life? Will life return to normal? How will I handle the "firsts"? Let's look at answers to each of these questions.

Who Am I?

You may have feelings of displacement. You may not be sure what your role is or where you fit anymore. Part of you is trying to hold on to your old identity (which is not possible), part of you is rebelling against any additional changes, and part of you wants to try to adjust to your new circumstances but has no idea how to do so. Some grieving people describe this as a feeling of having lost their identity.

Susan, whose daughter died suddenly after contracting meningitis, shares, "The first question with women is often 'How are your kids?' or 'What are your kids doing?' and my daughter was my only child. I felt so displaced in society. I couldn't even look at myself in the mirror for several months after she died. I didn't know who I was. I lost my identity."

As you are trying to adjust to your new reality, be careful not to choose grief as your new identity. Your grief and your loss should never define you. As Paul Tripp says, "Grief is a very significant human experience. It was never meant to be an identity. When I take it on as an identity, it will hurt me."

If you take on grief as your identity, you'll give yourself permission to isolate yourself, sleep away the days, let your responsibilities go, ignore your family—all the while telling yourself, "It's okay because I'm grieving." In the early days after the death, those actions are understandable, even encouraged, as you are in a state of shock and denial. But if you continue to live out those actions on a regular basis, you will never heal from your grief. You'll find that fewer and fewer people will want to spend time with you. And you'll never experience the amazing comfort God offers.

Thankfully, God has a better way for us to understand who we are—whether we're grieving or in the midst of one of the most joyous seasons of our lives. He wants us to know that our identity is in Christ.

Practically speaking, since our identity is in Christ, we should draw conclusions about ourselves from things the Bible tells us about Jesus and what he has done for us. Because the Bible tells us what will happen to Jesus in the future, our hopes and expectations are also impacted by truths about Christ. Using the example of a person who is depressed, Paul Tripp explains what a difference it makes knowing our identity is in Christ:

> A person who says, "I'm a depressed person," is saying that as an identity. Depression is a significant experience, but it's not an identity. If I take it on as an identity, it will hurt me because I will tend to give way to what that identity means. I'll say to myself, *Of course I'm sleeping more than I should; I'm depressed* and *Of course I've cut myself off from relationships; I'm depressed.* I'm giving myself permission because I've taken on that identity.
>
> Think about this statement, in contrast: "I am a child of the King of Kings and Lord of Lords. I have Jesus Christ living inside me. My God has promised to meet every one of my needs, and he is right here with me at this moment. By the way, I have a huge struggle with depression." Now I am keeping depression where it's a significant human experience, but it's not an identity.
>
> Grief is not an identity, and if I make it my identity, I'll start giving way to whatever definition of that identity I've given it. Grief is a profound experience to go through, and it rocks a person at the core. It's disruptive, dislocating, and highly emotional. But this experience doesn't define me. Christ defines me, and I now am a child of Christ in the midst of this particular experience.

How Will I Spend My Time?

As you begin to adjust to life in your new reality, you may discover that before the death, much of your time was centered on your loved one's interests, needs, and desires. You may have spent many hours driving a child to and from after-school lessons and activities, packing daily lunches, planning special gifts and surprises, playing together, and keeping your child's clothes clean. Perhaps you lovingly cared for an elderly parent by visiting, running errands, driving to doctor's appointments, and doing household chores.

If you lost your spouse, doing things he or she enjoyed was part of your relationship; you found pleasure in an activity for your spouse's sake. Trying to fit yourself into that mold now won't bring the same enjoyment because this is not a personal interest of yours.

> Every time I went someplace, I would ask myself, *Do I really like to do this? Or did I like to do it because Rick and I liked it together? Or was it because Rick liked it?* It came in bits and pieces as I sought to figure out who I was with Rick and then who I was without Rick. It was a process throughout the entire grief journey.
>
> I started defining things that I liked to do and my personality characteristics that I wanted to continue to embody. Using those personal discoveries, I began to put together the core of who Susan is now. Finally, I could say, "This is who I am. I am this whole, complete person." But it took a considerable length of time for that to happen, and it felt really good when I did know who I was.
>
> Susan Zonnebelt-Smeenge

Are you being disloyal if you stop doing things your loved one enjoyed? No, not in any way. Perhaps your loved one was a fan of a particular sport, and you spent many enjoyable times together in activities or discussion that revolved around that sport. Today, if that sport does not hold a strong personal

55

interest for you, you should not feel guilty about choosing not to watch or participate in that sport. Instead, you can enjoy sharing those memories with another person who does have that interest when those moments arise.

It's important that you renew some of your other interests and preferences. This is one of the best ways to make progress on your grief journey.

How Will I Adjust to My New Life?

You now live in what could be called your new reality. It's new, and it is reality. You didn't choose this, but because you are in it, you need to adjust to it in order to move forward and begin healing.

Part of living in this new reality involves having new responsibilities, new ways of doing things, new schedules, and new traditions. Some of your previous patterns will remain the same. Many will change. It's important to accept that these changes must come and then think about how you can function in this new normal.

Ask for Help with Responsibilities and Decision Making

"When my husband was alive, I'd say, 'We need an electrician; who do you want me to call?' Once he was gone, I didn't know what to do or who to call. That's when I needed to ask for help and find people who knew what they were doing. I learned to do that," shares Betty.

Choose to Do Some Things Differently

"Some people feel like they don't want to start new traditions because they're being disrespectful or disloyal to the person who's gone," says Lois Rabey, "but I don't agree with that. If your loved one could say something to you, he or she would say, 'I want you to go on living.' The reality is you can't re-create the same thing again anyway, and sometimes the pain of trying to re-create that old tradition without your loved one is greater than the pain of establishing a new tradition. New traditions are a good thing."

Take Small Steps to Adjust to Being on Your Own

"After the death of a spouse, you need to start to figure out how you're going to manage on your own, how you're going to be able to find some fulfillment in doing some things on your own," says Susan Zonnebelt-Smeenge. "It's a good thing to give oneself the assignment of 'maybe I will try to go out and see a movie by myself' or 'maybe I'll start by going to a fast-food restaurant and see what it feels like to go in by myself.' Those kinds of adjustments are very difficult, but they're also very fulfilling if you can leave saying, 'I did it, and I lived through it.' "

Will Life Return to Normal?

Since you have lost someone who will never return to you, unfortunately, life will not return to normal. But instead of longing for things to return to normal, you should prepare for a new normal.

> A new normal is sometimes starting new traditions, dropping traditions that don't work anymore or that are too painful to enter into. A new normal is thinking about my daughter in the past tense. A new normal is trying to keep her memory active, even though she is not here.
>
> Doug

> A new normal is accepting the fact that I no longer have a diaper baby; I went from having a toddler to my next child, who was then four years of age. A new normal is that we no longer have five boys; we only have four. It's hard to know

how to answer people when they ask me, "How many children do you have?" A new normal is accepting the fact that things will never be the same and gradually allowing your life to find a pattern again.

Sharon

I remember the first time I had to fill out an application, and I checked "married." Then I looked at it and thought, *No, I'm not married anymore. It was 'til death do us part.* I didn't want to put "single," and I definitely didn't want to put "widow." If I put "widow," it would just cement the fact that he was gone. But I scratched out "married," and I checked "widow."

Well, now it's normal. It's normal for me to check "widow." It's normal for me to be a single mom supporting my children.

Rochelle

Some people are concerned that they are being disloyal to their deceased loved one by trying to move forward or create a new normal. Think of it more as "How can I move forward in a way that honors the memory of my loved one?" As you walk forward day by day, carry special memories of your loved one with you and share them with other people, perhaps through a photograph or memento. Consider what character lessons and insights you learned from your loved one. Live them out, and pass them on to others.

Think about how much more those actions honor your loved one than constantly referring to how bad things are without your loved one or saying, "I can't do that new thing. My loved one and I never did it that way before." Choosing to remain stuck in your ways is not what God wants for you. And if you think about it, it's not what you really want for yourself.

It's important in the grief process to recognize that you have to have a new normal because the old normal will not return.

I spent a number of years thinking, *Sometime I'm going to feel normal again.* I finally realized I'm never going to feel like I did when Jack was alive because he's not here.

That fact alone means we have to have a new normal, and if you don't recognize that, you're trying to do something that's impossible to do. You can't go back. You can't relive the past, and if you're striving to do that, you're going to be continually frustrated.

Tell yourself and tell your children, if you have children, "It's never going to feel again like it felt when _____ was alive, but we're going to have a new normal, and that's going to be what we build the future on. Pain will be there, and it will be different, but with God's help we're going to have a full life and be blessed."

Lois Rabey

Grieving is never anything we "get over." We're meant to live in it and move through it, and out of that to live and be enlarged by that relationship and those experiences. And yes, we create a new normal.

Sandy

How Will I Handle the "Firsts"?

In your new reality, you will find yourself having to face many "firsts"—experiences you'll have to go through for the first time without your loved one. In the initial days after the death, the firsts are almost constant: first time sleeping at home without your loved one, first time waking up, first time eating breakfast, etc.

As the days and months go by, you'll experience other firsts. They are often highly emotional. The first time sitting at church without this person, first time grocery shopping, first time eating at a certain restaurant, first time taking a family picture. Holidays are particularly difficult because of the traditions you shared with this person.

Understand that these firsts will come, and sometimes they will surprise you, but you will need to face them. Robert DeVries shares:

> Almost everything you do after the death of a loved one you're going to do for the first time. Those firsts represent a constant reminder that your loved one is no longer with you. The firsts are also opportunities for you to say, "Okay, I'm going to do this once. This is going to hurt. It may be an emotional trauma for me to do this." I would encourage you to do it then a second time and even a third time.

You can do this, but don't feel you have to face everything all at once. Take your time. As you encounter each first, invite God to be your strength by boasting in your weakness, as Paul advises in 2 Corinthians 12:9.

A Word of Encouragement

We've offered suggestions and advice so far throughout this book, and you may feel a bit discouraged thinking you have so much grief work to do. Please understand you are not meant to travel this journey of grief on your own. Friends, family members, church people, grief support group friends, counselors, and pastors are here on this earth to help you. Most importantly, God never runs out of time, energy, patience, or strength. He is real, and he will comfort and strengthen you during these difficult changes. He alone can bring you the peace and comfort you need to make it through the days ahead. Turn to him and allow him to help you.

7

Dealing with
Insensitive Comforters

People around us don't understand grief unless they've been
through it themselves.

H. Norman Wright

Be patient with each other, making allowance for each other's
faults because of your love.

Ephesians 4:2 NLT

At times when people seek to comfort you, what they
do or say may cause you to feel worse. This chapter
provides ideas on ways to respond when faced with
these awkward, hurtful moments.

Why Comfort Goes Wrong

Unfortunately, as people seek to comfort you, they may
actually hurt you. This feels frustrating and unfair because,

after all, you are already suffering enough! But it's reality. Knowing why these awkward, painful moments occur will prepare you to deal with them. That knowledge will also keep you from losing friends as you deal with your loss. Plus, it will give you the opportunity to extend the same mercy and love to others that God has shown to you.

People Are Inexperienced Comforters

Few people sit around thinking of ways to offend grieving people. So why does it happen so much? One reason is that many comforters have never experienced a loss before, so they have no idea how to care for you. You're often being comforted by a rookie, and he or she is probably afraid you'll get upset or make a scene when spoken to. That combination of fear, inexperience, and a sincere desire to help often leads to awkward moments.

People Misuse Scripture

Normally, we want to hear from God. His words are encouraging and refreshing. They are a source of hope. Unfortunately, not everyone knows how to use God's Word wisely. People may hit you over the head with Scripture passages taken out of context. They may also share passages that are too much for you to process at this point in your grief.

Barbara Johnson, who founded a grief ministry, says, "After the death of one of my sons, people would come over and tell me, 'How wonderful that he's in heaven; isn't it wonderful?' I didn't feel that way then. They had a lot of words to say, and they quoted Scripture. I wasn't ready for that."

Wendy shares, "Sometimes people would say, 'You just need to trust in God.' At times I wanted to stand up and say, 'I know that. I got that part, okay? I know I'm supposed to trust in God, and it still feels just as bad today as it felt yesterday.' "

If this happens, understand that your comforters mean well. Don't use those incidents to form a negative opinion about God's Word. Again, the problem is usually the poor judgment or timing of the one who's quoting it. At a later date you may be comforted or encouraged by those same words.

People Are Following the Golden Rule

Another reason comfort can go wrong is that people often assume what is helpful for them will be helpful to you. In a sense, you can't fault them. To the best of their abilities, they're following the Golden Rule: doing unto others as they would have someone do unto them. Sue Lutz, family counselor, explains how this dynamic works—or doesn't.

> People revert to their default mode, which is, "What helps me?" Those people might not be the same kind of person you are, so what helps them may not necessarily help you. If they give you tickets to a musical performance that they would like, and you don't like that kind of music, it's an empty gesture. If you like to clean your house and it's therapeutic for you, and somebody comes and offers to clean your house, it's not going to accomplish the intended purpose. It's important for you to be forthright and let them know what helps and what does not.

Help Your Comforters Comfort You

Have Mercy on Them

In helping your comforters comfort you, start by having mercy on them. When you are tempted to condemn their callous words or actions, remind yourself of how you would have acted in the same situation—before your personal experience with grief. Even if you would not have acted or spoken in the same way, understand that your comforters are not intentionally seeking to hurt you. They are doing the best they know to do.

Lois and Sharon were both hurt by a comment from a well-meaning person. In response, both women made wise decisions on how to handle the situation.

Lois Rabey shares:

> One day at church a woman came up to me and took me by the shoulders and shook me and said, "You need to cry." I wanted to yell at her, "I cry all the time," but I didn't, and I went on. I avoided her for a while. I was upset with her and would walk the other way when I saw her.
>
> Then I stopped one day, and I thought, *You know what? She meant well. She didn't realize what she was doing and how invasive it was. I need to just let that go. I don't need to say anything to her about it, but I need to stop avoiding her, and I need to be kind to her.*
>
> People do mean well. They're very uncomfortable, and they don't know what to say. Sometimes they put their foot in their mouth. We need to be gracious and say, "Thanks" and go on.

Sharon, who lost her two-year-old son, shares:

> At my son's funeral a woman came to me and said, "Well, at least you won't have to potty train him." That was really, really hurtful, and it made me angry. But I talked with her later because I felt she should know that those kinds of things are not acceptable to say to a grieving mother. She asked forgiveness, and we have a good relationship.

When it's difficult to muster up the strength to have mercy on insensitive comforters, remind yourself of how merciful and kind God has been to you. The Bible tells us that we offend God in many ways, and we were once his enemies—yet he still made a great sacrifice to show his love and care for us (Eph. 2:1–3). We should do the same to others.

Evaluate Your Expectations of Your Comforters

It's a good idea to evaluate the expectations you have of people. Why? If you don't, your unrealistic expectations may ruin some of your relationships. So ask yourself, *What am I expecting from people? Do I have certain expectations of certain people?* It may bother you for one person to make a certain comment, but you wouldn't be offended to hear that same remark from someone else. Take a moment to jot down what you really expect and desire from specific people around you.

Consider whether your expectations are a bit ambitious for the people you are assigning them to. Perhaps that person has never experienced a loss. Maybe that person does not have the maturity to think carefully before speaking or to apologize when he or she has gone too far. You may need to lower your expectations of certain people. Also, do not hesitate to let those people know when their words or actions are hurtful. You could say, "I do appreciate your trying to help, but actually that wasn't very helpful. It hurt my feelings. Perhaps next time you could do or say this . . . That would help a lot."

For close friends, you will want to clearly communicate your expectations. Don't quietly wait for them to do or say the right thing. This is unfair because it puts them in the position of having to read your mind. Since your grief is unique, it's unlikely that anyone will know exactly what you need said or done.

Let Others Know What Is Helpful

It may be frustrating, not to mention exhausting, that *you* have to take the time to help others understand what you need. But this is part of living with grief. It's part of the healing, coping process. Plus, if you don't, you're setting yourself up for more awkward, painful moments. Therefore,

65

communicating with your comforters—be it through a spoken conversation, a letter, or an email—is wise. You won't have a great deal of energy to reach out to others, but find a way that works for you. Let your comforters know:

- what helps
- what doesn't help
- the truth about how you are feeling
- how thankful you are for their friendship

With so many people asking, "How are you doing?" "How can I help?" it may seem easier to say, "I'm fine," and move on. This isn't the best way to respond to your potential comforters. H. Norman Wright advises:

> When someone asks you how you're doing, be honest. "I'm having a difficult day. I've really been struggling today. Today on a scale of 0 to 10, I'm probably at a 3, but I appreciate your asking."
>
> A gentleman I've worked with put a different message on his answering machine every week for four years. His friends would hear things like, "Hi, this is Dave. I'm struggling today because I'm really feeling the loss of my wife," or "Today has been a little better, and I'd like to share this Scripture with you." For four years his friends were taught the journey of grief through Dave telling his ups and his downs on his message system.

You can let people know what's going on, how you are feeling, and how to best comfort you through whatever method works best for you—whether in person, on your voice mail message, or another avenue. As your strength returns, and as you put some of the ideas in this book into practice, you will become more comfortable expressing your feelings and needs, and you'll be better able to gain comfort from your relationships.

A Word of Encouragement

Letting people know what you need and how to comfort you during your grief is important. It will make things easier for both you and the people trying to help you. We encourage you to be patient with their mistakes and graciously accept the comfort you do receive. And keep talking with God because he can help on both sides of your relationships.

8

Your Grieving Family

A healthy way to respond to grief is to recognize that all
your family members are grieving at their own pace and in
their own way.

Susan Beeney, RN

Put [your] religion into practice by caring for [your] own
family . . . for this is pleasing to God.

1 Timothy 5:4

Your family members are all expressing grief in their own
way, and this can be tough for you as you seek to care
for your family, as well as grieve your own grief. This
chapter will help you understand different grieving styles and
will guide you in helping your family through grief.

Don't Expect Family Members to Grieve the Same Way

David and Nancy Guthrie, co-hosts of the GriefShare support
group program, experienced the death of two of their three

children. They found that figuring out how to share their grief and then to accept each other's way of grieving was difficult. On top of that, Nancy shares, "We also had to help our son process the loss of his brother and sister. Since we were so sad, this was often hard to do. It required a lot of effort to work through the process of grief in a way that made our family stronger."

The experience of working through grief can actually draw your family closer. It can even make your bonds stronger. But expecting family members to grieve the same way creates conflict.

Nancy continues, "I learned that when I was sad, it was impossible, in my eyes, for David to do the right thing. I knew it hurt him to see me suffering. But if he began comforting me, I felt pressure to stop crying. If he ignored me, it hurt my feelings. He couldn't win."

David shares his viewpoint: "If I'm honest, I'd have to admit that sometimes Nancy's brokenness scared me. I wondered if I'd ever get my old wife back. And being unable to take away her pain left me feeling helpless. Thankfully, early in our grieving process I was counseled to 'let Nancy be sad.' That proved to be valuable advice."

You may feel that a family member does not seem to be grieving as much as you are, but it is likely that the person is. He or she just doesn't express grief or cope with it the way you do. Why? Your response to grief depends on factors such as your personality, your background, prior experiences with loss, how grieving and coping have been modeled for you, and how willing you are to face and work through your grief. Just as you don't want others to critique the manner in which you grieve, extend that same grace to those around you.

Children Grieve Differently than Adults

Your children face many of the same emotions you do, but often they face emotions you have no idea they are experiencing. Unfortunately, children do not know what to do with their grief. Someone must tell them what to do and show them how to do it. You probably won't have the energy and focus needed to give your children the care they need. This is why it's good to have another adult around who is willing to help your children deal with their grief. Consider asking a close relative or family friend to read this chapter and to spend time helping your children.

Whoever cares for your children during this time needs to be aware of the typical emotions grieving children face. Here are a few of the most common ones.

Guilt. You may be surprised to know that your children may blame themselves for causing your loved one's death. For instance, if they were unkind or refused to do something the loved one had asked recently, they may take the blame upon themselves. You may need to explain repeatedly to them how and why your loved one died.

Anger. They may be angry at their loved one for dying and leaving them alone. They may be angry at their loved one for causing so much change and causing you to be so sad. They may direct their anger toward you.

Fear and anxiety. Your children may fear you will never be happy again and that their household will never be a safe, happy home again. They may fear that you or another family member will die. To keep you from being sad, your children may not cry in front of you. This is another reason it's important for your children to have an adult friend or family member with whom they can share their feelings.

One difference between grieving adults and children is that children grieve intermittently. Whereas adults feel they are constantly flailing in a tidal wave of emotions, children will experience those strong emotions and then take a break. The next thing you know, they're playing with their friends, laughing, and having fun. Recognize that your children are grieving and be there to help, but also allow your children to be children.

How to Help Grieving Children

Model Grief

To help grieving children, start by modeling how to express grief. For instance, if you experienced a certain emotion today, tell your children about that emotion. "Today I heard _____'s favorite song on the radio. It made me feel sad, and I cried. Did something happen to you today that reminded you of _____?" By having that conversation, you are (1) showing your children how to define an emotion, (2) letting them know it's okay to talk about those emotions, and (3) letting them know it's okay to cry and to feel that emotion.

Share Emotions through Artwork and Play

Give your children opportunities to express their emotions and hurts through artwork. Set out paper and crayons, or make homemade play dough. Ask your children about what they are creating. Sit down with your children and draw a special memory of your loved one. Or create something that will remind your children that they are special, loved, and wanted.

Blocks, LEGOs®, and other building toys are good tools for expressing thoughts and emotions through play. Ask them questions about their creation and use that discussion as a springboard for talking about memories and emotions. Another idea is to set out your children's dolls or action figures in the living room while you work nearby. Then keep your ears open for play conversations that may reveal what the children are struggling with.

Find Comfort through Sight, Touch, and Smell

Some children prefer to express their grief using their senses of sight, touch, and smell. Allow your children to choose an object of your loved one's to sleep with or carry with them. Perhaps your children would like to wear a hat, shirt, or piece of jewelry your loved one used to wear. This brings them a sense of comfort. Is there a certain scent your loved one wore? Let the children spray that scent on their pillow or in their room.

Teach Your Children to Seek God's Help

If you want your children to seek God's help as they grieve, it will be helpful for them to observe you in your pursuit of God. Allow your children to join you for prayer or to sit with you as you read the Bible. You don't have to teach during these times. Your children will learn volumes by seeing you make time to draw strength and encouragement from God.

Also, frequently remind your children why God can be trusted, despite the fact that he allows us to experience pain. Let them know that God has demonstrated his love for us by sending Christ to suffer for our sins. Explain to them that while their grief hurts now, Christ's death means that eventually everything will be all right and that one day there will be no more pain or suffering.

Talk to Them about Death

When you talk to your children about death, it's important to use truthful, age-appropriate language. Avoid abstract euphemisms. For example, telling children "Grandpa has gone on a long journey" isn't helpful. The next time you tell your children you're going on a long trip, they may conclude you're about to die. Depending on the age of the children, you may be able to say something as simple as, "Grandpa's body stopped working, and now he is in heaven." If your children have more questions about what it means to die, H. Norman Wright advises you to speak in short, simple statements that communicate what death is and that it is permanent. He gives an example: "Death means Grandfather won't be able to do what he used to do. He won't be able to talk. He won't be able to feel. He won't be able to walk. He can't eat or drink. He doesn't breathe anymore. His body is no longer going to be here."

Norm continues, "You need to give as much information as the children can handle according to their age level, and you've got to be honest."

Spouses Grieve Differently

After the death of their daughter, Doug and Ann grieved differently and found comfort in different places, but they also found a way to accept those differences, which helped them heal personally and as a couple.

Ann says:

> We knew we were different, and we were able to respect each other's differences. If there were things he needed to do to help him grieve that did not help me, it was okay. If there were things I needed to do that he didn't, it was okay. He enjoyed going to the cemetery. That did nothing for me. There was a video we had from the funeral service that I looked at every week for at least two years. He's only seen that video once.

Doug shares:

> We never beat each other up about this. I never came back and said, "Why aren't you going to the cemetery?" and she never said, "Why don't you sit down and watch this video?" We never set any kind of a timetable either. I never said to Ann, "Don't you think it's about time you stopped watching this video?" We respected each other's territory. But there were days we came home and just looked at each other, and we literally fell into each other's arms. We would cry, not a word spoken, but we knew right there that we were 100 percent together on this.

Sometimes you may feel critical of your spouse for not handling grief the way you think it should be handled. Instead of judging, talk with your spouse about what you are feeling and what brings you comfort. After you listen to one another, reassure your spouse that you understand that your way of grieving will likely be different from his/hers and that's okay. Make sure your spouse knows you are committed to your marriage even though the road ahead will be extremely tough.

Everyone needs to talk about and express grief, but not everyone will do this in the same way or want to do it at the same time. If you are unable to share your grief with your spouse at this time, find a same-sex friend whom you can open up with and who will be encouraging and supportive. But as you grow this same-sex friendship, remember that your spouse needs you to remain committed to the marriage and present in the marriage. You can't run off every time you need to talk and your spouse is unwilling.

If you're a Christian, God expects you to love and respect your spouse the way Christ loved you. Just as Christ made sacrifices that benefit you, you must make sacrifices to do what is in your spouse's best interest. In this situation, that may mean making sacrifices of your time or preferences. You may have to change what, and how much, you are willing to endure from your spouse as he or she grieves.

Always be careful about the words you say to your spouse or to another grieving family member. Words said in the heat of emotion cannot be taken back and are difficult to recover from. Proverbs 12:18 says, "Reckless words pierce like a sword, but the tongue of the wise brings healing." Knowing that another person may be grieving differently than you can help keep you from judging and criticizing, since you really don't know what's going on in that person's heart.

Managing a Grieving Family

You may feel like you are drowning in sorrow and have nothing to offer, but withdrawal is not an option. If you have a family, they need you. So how can you manage your grieving family when you can barely manage your own grief? Seek God's help daily.

"Often you are so deep in grief that it's hard to meet the needs of the rest of your family," says Kristi, who, after her son's death, had two other children at home and a husband to care for. "I realized quickly that I needed to spend more time with God, allowing him to pull me up, and I needed to devote time to doing what I needed to do for my family. I had to stretch myself in a way that's hard and just stick it out."

Rest assured that God knows and dearly loves each person in your family, and he'll give you the strength and the ability to help each other. God understands that you need to grieve, but he also put you in a family, and you each have roles to fulfill as a part of this family.

Your roles may change after the death of a family member. An important step in defining and communicating these new family roles is to plan a family meeting. Discuss which family members will take over new tasks or gaps in chores created by the death. Acknowledge that things will be different around the house and that some responsibilities may be painful to do, but they must be done. Communicate that you will learn together how to function in this new normal, this new family structure, and that you will do it together, with God as your stable center. You may want to take this time to lead the family in a prayer, asking God to help each person in your family.

Signs Your Family Is Grieving in a Healthy Manner

If a family is healthy when there's a loss in the family, they're going to talk about it. They're going to face it. They're going to encourage one another to grieve in their own way and at their own pace. They're not going to put restrictions on one another.

Sometimes, you find family members who will say, "You can talk about it, but just not around me" or "Go to your room when you are showing your emotion because it will upset other people." Those things don't happen in a healthy family. Healthy families are going to look out for one another and not just for themselves.

H. Norman Wright

To facilitate healthy family grieving, make sure your family members are aware of their grief support options. Gather information about local grief support groups for all ages. Look for age-appropriate Christian books on grief-related topics. Find local Christian counselors for family members who may prefer this option. Talk to pastors, friends, relatives, or church members who might be willing to come alongside particular family members as mentors, listeners, and prayer support. Encourage your family to take advantage of the help that's available.

Cry Out to the Lord for Help

> Hear my prayer, LORD,
>   listen to my cry for help;
>   do not be deaf to my weeping. (Ps. 39:12)

The burden of helping and managing your grieving family is not yours to bear on your own. God dearly loves and will help each individual in your family. Cry out to him for help for yourself and your family members.

The following individuals share practical ideas of how to cry out to God and find help and comfort:

There's no way you can deal with all those emotions. The best way is to cry out to God. God is big enough to handle everything we have to give him.

For me, crying out means doing something physical, using my lungs, using my voice, and really telling God how I feel. We had a treadmill on the third floor, and when everyone was gone from the house, I would go up there and run as hard as I could and scream as loud as I could, and no one could hear me but God. It brought great relief.

Kristi

Reading through the Psalms was a tremendous help. The Scriptures are full of comfort from the Lord.

Sharon

People have called Psalm 88 the "psalm of the dark night of the soul." The writer, Heman, is a wise, godly man who shares his despair, doubt, and confusion with God, and he ends with the words, "The darkness is my closest friend."

I challenge people to write a song about their dark night of the soul. Sometimes Christians feel like they have to tack on, "And thank you, God, for all your blessings." Heman didn't feel that need because he understood the nature of biblical complaint: it's being honest with God about your faith and doubt. It shows you believe that God cares and can handle everything about you.

Robert Kellemen, counselor

A Word of Encouragement

Pray for your grieving family. God wants to be there for each of you and to provide for the needs of each family member. You might like to pray this prayer:

Father God, my pain is so deep, and my family is suffering around me. But I can barely cope with my own hurts, much less look out for those I love. Please help me to give my burdens to you consistently and to accept your help, comfort, provision, and guidance. Give each of us enough grace to make it through every new day as it comes. Grant me the wisdom not only to make good decisions concerning my own daily life but also to be wise about decisions affecting my family.

9

Making Sense
of Your Situation

We think if we had an answer, then we'd be more in control.

H. Norman Wright

When I tried to understand all this,
    it troubled me deeply
till I entered the sanctuary of God;
    then I understood their final destiny.

Psalm 73:16–17

As you try to make sense of your situation, this chapter will help you reframe your perspective of what you're going through in light of God's story.

Your story probably goes something like this: "My loved one has died. At times it feels like my life is over. I hurt so badly; sometimes I don't think I'll make it." Whenever you reflect on how your story has played out, you're left crying out, "Why? Why me? Why my loved one? Why now?"

While God invites us to ask him questions, many who've gone through grief have found that God gives us something greater than answers to our questions: he gives us himself. Joseph Stowell, president of Cornerstone University, says, "When we look at our problem through God, we may not get direct answers to our questions on this side of life, but the answers reside in who God is in his character, in what we know to be true about God."

You Must Understand God's Story

Imagine you're at a friend's retirement ceremony. His family, friends, and co-workers have joined to celebrate his forty-plus years in the workforce. As you listen to tribute after tribute, you take notice of his beautiful wife of thirty-five years, and you realize that though he's the one being celebrated, the events of his life story have had, and will have, an impact on his wife and family. For example, every time he received a promotion, the family benefited by having more money in the budget. When he had to move, the family was affected as well. Now that he's retired, he'll be able to spend more time with his wife, travel more, and spend more time with his grandkids. So the events of his life have significantly affected and will affect the lives of others.

In the same way, we benefit from events (past, present, and future) that are found in God's story. What many who've grieved have discovered is that the events of God's story directly affect us. And the more you understand the details of God's story and how it affects you, the better equipped you are to make sense of your grief experience.

What Is God's Story?

God's story reveals God's character, his goals, his plan for the world. In it he gently introduces us to a different perspective of what we're going through. If you take the time to get to know God's story, the horrible turn that your story has taken will slowly begin to make sense, and you will discover the reason for hope for both you and your loved one.

> The story is that God created a perfect world, a gorgeous beautiful world, and in the center of that world he placed two human beings whom he had made, Adam and Eve. Their job was to take care of this world that he had created. Adam and Eve decided to rebel against God because they bought the lie that they could be like gods. What that brought into the world was sin, and sin is the breaking of all the good things God has created.
>
> So we live in this broken world, this world that doesn't operate the way it's supposed to, and we don't operate the way we're supposed to. We don't think, speak, or act the way we're supposed to.
>
> God wasn't content for that to happen, so he sent his Son, the Lord Jesus Christ, not only to provide forgiveness but also to enable us to live the way we were meant to live and to make the whole world new. We're in the middle of the story because we're not completely made new yet, and the world isn't completely made new yet, but there will be a day when that will happen.
>
> Paul Tripp

That, in short, is God's story, as explained in the Bible. It's likely that the first two acts of God's story parallel your story of grief: once things were great, and now that your loved one is gone, they're not. But here's where the story of the Bible helps us reframe our stories. Even though the story of the Bible reaches a point of despair, it concludes gloriously, and your story can too. In fact, your story is part of the story of the Bible. That's why God's story is the perfect story to help you make sense of what is happening to you now and to give you a reason for hope.

What Does His Story Have to Do with Me?

Your personal story is part of a much larger story—a story that is still in progress but that has an amazingly wonderful ending. Trying to understand what you're going through, without seeing it in light of God's story, produces frustration, despair, and hopelessness.

> God's story has a beginning and it has an end, and it has a plot that's going somewhere. Because my story is a piece of that, it can't possibly be out of control—maybe out of my control, but it's not out of God's control. Even though I don't understand what is going on in this moment, even though things are messy and chaotic and confusing, what I'm going through right now is part of a bigger story. That means everything I'm facing has meaning and purpose even though I may not be able to figure that out at this moment.
>
> Paul Tripp

"God's story says that death is an episode within his larger story. It certainly takes seriously the tragedy of death, but it says, 'Come with me now, and let's look at the end of the story,'" explains Edward Welch. "The end of the story is a place where there will be no more tears and no more crying, where there will be unity and perfect love, and death will be conquered.

"How can we understand that that's the story line we are in a sense asked to become a part of? We have to adopt his view of life rather than our own. That demands a good bit of humility. It demands a trust in him. It demands that we lay down our arms and give up our anger with God and accept that he does have a plan. That's what faith is."

When we, by faith, see our stories as part of God's story, we discover comforting and eye-opening truths that help us make sense of our suffering. Let's look at each one in detail.

God Has a Plan

God's original plan was for a world of perfection, production, unity, and peace—no sorrow, no death. But instead of living within the parameters of safety, peace, obedience, and joy, Adam and Eve gave in to the temptation to be like gods themselves.

81

The resulting sin and brokenness and separation from God that Adam and Eve experienced also affect us. How? All the sickness, death, and violence we experience share a common root: Adam and Eve's rebellion against God. But God has already set a plan in motion through his Son Jesus to overcome the pain, brokenness, and consequences of sin once and for all. This means that God has a plan for what's happening to you.

God Is in Control

Although you have no control over the fact that your loved one died and the consequences occurring in the aftermath, this does not mean the situation is out of control. God never loses control of a situation.

If you are riding in an airplane and the airplane has to make an emergency landing because of equipment failure, your emotions and physical sense of well-being are a mess and you have no control over what's happening, but you are well aware that you'd rather have a trained pilot in control than you. God is a pilot who knows all aspects of the situation, who never makes a mistake, and who always guides you into a safe landing. Having faith in God will allow you to trust God in the midst of your suffering, even though you don't have the answers to all your questions.

All the days ordained for me were written in your book before one of them came to be. (Ps. 139:16)

My times are in your hands. (Ps. 31:15)

By knowing God's story, you know that God is in control—even though it may not feel like it. It's important to come to the point where you say, "I may not understand it, but I choose to trust that you are in control and that your plan is for the ultimate good of both my loved one and me." Being able to make the above declaration, however, does not come overnight. The more you get to know God's character, the more you will come to embrace and trust in this truth.

God Never Promised a Pain-Free Life

Picture a family with two teenage children. It's November, and they've just found out their dad unexpectedly lost his job. The weeks go by and he has no prospects. As the teens look toward Christmas, they know they can't expect all the fun games and gifts and treats of the past. They understand they need to have proper expectations of that day so they won't be confused, angry, or disappointed.

We have certain expectations in every situation, but when we have the right expectations for the situation at hand, that makes it easier to face and to handle what's happening. God's story helps us set proper expectations about what's promised in this life. It tells us that we live in a broken world. We will experience pain. Why? Because we are in the middle of God's story. At some point our world will be renewed, and evil and death will be no more, but right now those of us on earth live in the brokenness of sin and death.

The Bible says God cares about each one of us, and he is the Father of comfort. Everyone experiences pain. Everyone goes through dark times. It's a normal part of life in this world. The difference is that you can have someone comforting, strengthening, and guiding you through the darkness. The difference is that you can make it through the darkness because you hope in a greater promise, a better life, and a God who will never leave your side.

> Brothers and sisters, we do not want you to be uninformed about those who sleep in death, so that you do not grieve like the rest of mankind, who have no hope. (1 Thess. 4:13)

There Is Reason for Hope

Although we are in the middle of the story, we have the promise that this story will come to an end and that "there will be no more death or mourning or crying or pain, for the old order of things has passed away. He who was seated on the throne said, 'I am making everything new!' " (Rev. 21:4–5). Isaiah 25:8–9 says, "He will swallow up death forever. The Sovereign LORD will wipe away the tears from all faces. . . . In that day they will say, 'Surely this is our God; we trusted in him, and he saved us.' "

You can never be defeated by death and suffering if you've chosen to walk with Christ and look toward the glorious conclusion of God's story. We can look forward to this new life today and every day!

Patricia shares what she learned about hope after the death of her husband and her two sons:

> Being hopeful doesn't mean that we don't hurt or cry or that we forget our loved ones. It doesn't mean we wouldn't go back if we could and change it to where they were still here. Being hopeful means trusting that the Lord knows best. It means that when I do get sad, I can get down on my knees or I can sit before him and say, "God, I'm hurting today. I need an extra dose of your love. I don't understand. I accept, but I don't understand." This means relying totally on him and knowing he is going to provide.

Our prayer for you as you seek to walk forward in grief, with God by your side, is this: "May the God of hope fill you with all joy and peace as you trust in him, so that you may overflow with hope by the power of the Holy Spirit" (Rom. 15:13).

A Word of Encouragement

God is so kind to tell us that he has a plan to deal with suffering and death. While this won't change the fact that you are grieving, it is a reason for hope. Ask God to help you find comfort in the answers he gives you. Thank him for his willingness to disclose his plans to you.

10

How Your Thinking Shapes Your Grief

When you come up against your expectations and your assumptions about how life is supposed to work, God says, "Let's look at what you think life is about versus what I say." If your heart is soft to the Lord, then you say, "Lord, I am so out of my league; you have to teach me."

Sue Lutz

"For my thoughts are not your thoughts,
neither are your ways my ways," declares the LORD.
"As the heavens are higher than the earth,
so are my ways higher than your ways
and my thoughts than your thoughts."

Isaiah 55:8–9

Learning to have an accurate interpretation of what's happening to you is key to grieving with hope.

Let's say today is your birthday. You sit down at the breakfast table, but no one says a word. "What are the plans for today?" you ask and are met with shrugs and incoherent responses. Arriving at work you see a cream-colored envelope on your desk. *Aha!* you think. But it's only an announcement for an office event. As the day goes by, your phone remains silent and your feelings of hurt begin to come out as sharp, impatient retorts to your co-workers. Finally, at night, you wearily open the front door of your house . . . and are met with a chorus of "Surprise!" plus streamers, balloons, and laughing faces.

Based on what you saw, heard, and were experiencing, you completely misinterpreted the situation and drew the wrong conclusions. You *thought* your conclusions were correct, but they were not. Once you had more information and had broadened your perspective, you realized there was much more going on than you'd originally understood.

Interpreting Your Experiences

You respond to and draw conclusions about every experience based on your interpretation of what you see, hear, and believe to be true. Sometimes what you think is true, or what feels true, is not true at all.

Your interpretation is the driving force behind how you respond to your loss. If you are coming to the wrong conclusions about what is happening to you, your resulting behavior will prevent your healing. "I've met many people who have been through virtually identical experiences," says Sue Lutz, "but their responses take them in completely different directions because of what they decided their experience meant about them, about God, about life, their future, and their purpose."

If you reflect on the death of your loved one and interpret it to mean, "I'm alone. No one cares for me or understands how I feel, and God has deserted me," then you will act accordingly. You won't want to spend time with other people. You won't be motivated to read the Bible. You'll see no point in going to church. Prayer will seem pointless. Unfortunately, by rejecting those things, you cut yourself off from the resources you need to heal—all because you've misinterpreted what's happening to you. As Paul Tripp says, grief may block your ability to see God, but "you should not conclude that means he is absent."

We encourage you to speak God's truth to yourself. Doing so will help you interpret what's happening to you in a way that will help you heal.

No one is more important in your life than you are because nobody talks to you more than you do. In moments of grief, you are involved in this unending internal conversation, and what you tell yourself is terribly important. You've got to tell yourself, "Although I feel alone, although there are people who say they love me who haven't shown up for me in this moment, although I don't feel God's presence, he is with me."

Paul Tripp

How to Interpret Your Experiences Accurately

To interpret your experiences correctly, you have to know the truth.

Remind Yourself of Where You Live

One way to tell yourself the truth about what is happening is to remind yourself of what the Bible says about where you live—not your neighborhood but your world. As we saw in the previous chapter, the Bible, God's story, teaches us that, while beautiful, our world has been marred by sin, so there is suffering. People are killed in earthquakes, people are murdered, and our bodies fail. But as devastating as these events can be and as shocked as we may be by the timing of them, in another sense, we should not be surprised that things of this nature occur.

Reminding yourself of where you live helps you remember that suffering in this life is normal. While this truth doesn't lessen the pain, it keeps you from interpreting what's happened to you as some sort of raw deal from God. Instead, you see that God is trustworthy because he's warned you that this life is marked by suffering.

Reminding yourself of where you live also helps you remember that the best experiences and relationships this life has to offer were never meant to be permanent. While we enjoy what God offers us in this life, we must also remember we are not experiencing the best possible reality. God wants us to look forward to a time when he will make all things new and usher in a world exempt from sorrow.

Spend Time with God's Word

Another thing you should do is remind yourself of the specific ways God cares for you. One way to do this is to write down Bible verses and post them in places where you'll see them and read them throughout each day. Carry verses in your wallet, pockets, or handbag. Keep them on your computer desktop. Play music that incorporates Bible verses and that focuses on God's truths.

God says, "I have given you my words in the Bible so that you have a way to leave behind interpretations of life that keep you far from me and steer you in a destructive direction." Let God's promises be specifically applied to your situation. That's how you get traction, move forward, have healing, and have a bigger perspective on what God wants to accomplish in you, through you, and for you in your grief.

Sue Lutz

Think about What Is Good

Finally, to understand the truth that not everything is bad in your life, take note of all the good things that are happening to you, even momentary good events. Did you see something that made you genuinely smile this week? Did you experience the love of a friend or relative? Is the sky blue today? Did your pet give you a loving nuzzle? Noticing good moments is a great way to apply Philippians 4:8: "Fix your thoughts on what is true, and honorable, and right, and pure, and lovely, and admirable. Think about things that are excellent and worthy of praise" (NLT).

One thing that can help you see your situation differently is to grow in your appreciation for how much God loves you. If you find yourself wondering why God would allow you to experience so much pain, remind yourself of this: God loves you so much that he allowed his Son to take the punishment, on the cross, for your sins to spare you from everlasting suffering. While your pain now is very great, the Bible says that the pain God has spared us from, through Christ's death on the cross, is far greater than any pain we'll ever experience in this life. That's why Romans says, "Blessed is the one whose sin the Lord will never count against them" (4:8). What's more, if God was willing to give his Son for us, he must be willing to give us the comfort we need. That's why later in the book of Romans we read, "He who did not spare his own Son, but gave him up for us all—how will he not also, along with him, graciously give us all things?" (8:32).

Rose-Colored Glasses?

By suggesting that you think honestly about what is good and what is true in relation to your situation, you may wonder if we're asking you to downplay the seriousness of your loss, or if thinking about what is good is like asking you to put on rose-colored glasses. Robert Kellemen says that looking at a situation with spiritual eyes (seeing what is good and true) is far different from looking at life through rose-colored glasses: "In rose-colored glasses I say life is good, and I deny the reality that life is bad. With spiritual eyes I say life is bad but God is good, and there is a world of difference between those."

If you were to say that everything happening to you is good, that would be a wrong interpretation. God says there are such things as evil and suffering. We should not act as if those things do not exist. An accurate interpretation acknowledges that good and bad things happen.

How to Tell if Your Thinking Is on Track

One way to tell if you're being honest about your grief—if you're interpreting your experiences accurately—is to listen to the way you talk about what's happening to you. So if, when talking to others about your situation, you sound like someone who realizes life is bad but God is good, you're likely interpreting your situation correctly and are on your way to making it through your grief.

Siang-Yang Tan describes what a person who grasps this truth sounds like and what someone who does not grasp this truth sounds like. Which person sounds most like you?

> If you've lost your spouse and you say things like, "It's the end of the world. I cannot go on. I miss him/her so much. This person was everything to me," your words are extremely negative. As a result, you'll be in your depression and your sadness much longer.
>
> But suppose you say things like, "I miss my spouse. I really long for him/her. I'm sad. I'm depressed. I'm not sure how I'm going to be able to cope with this, but I know God will make a way for me. I know it's not the end of the world. I know God will give me grace sufficient for the day. I know I have friends who will support me and pray for me. I know I can talk to a counselor and my pastor." You're now talking in a biblical, healthier way.

A Word of Encouragement

As you can see, your experience of grief is shaped by the thinking you bring to it. That's why Paul Tripp says, "We don't live life based on the facts of our experience, but we live life based on our interpretations of the facts." God is good to help you reinterpret your daily happenings. Without his enlightenment, you will continue to interpret situations based on your experience and knowledge. Doing so will keep you from being able to move forward and to fully accept his comfort. We encourage you to embrace God's perspective of what's happening to you.

11

Forgiving Those Responsible for the Death

God says that forgiving is the way to protect yourself from bearing a weight that only he can carry.

Sue Lutz

If you, LORD, kept a record of sins,
 Lord, who could stand?
But with you there is forgiveness.

Psalm 130:3–4

As you are trying to walk forward in hope, you may still be facing other obstacles, such as feelings of anger and blame. This can create barriers against the peace God wants to fill you with. This chapter will help you understand the role forgiveness plays in healing from your grief.

Struggling to Forgive?

Joanne's son died in a car accident. The vehicle he was riding in hit a weed-sprayer truck parked on the side of the road. She shares honestly, "I swore I would never forgive the person who was driving the car or the guy who had the truck on the side of the road who wasn't doing his job according to the law. I also believed my son was taken from me because of sins I had committed, my actions, and my lack of faith in God. I was angry. I was unforgiving."

Like Joanne, you may blame a person, a group, or a company for your loved one's death. But even if an individual or group is responsible for your loved one's death, refusing to forgive won't help you recover from your grief. In fact, not forgiving hurts you now and in eternity. Refusing to forgive can shape you into a person you don't want to be: a bitter person, one who keeps a record of wrongs, one who's not able to love and serve others freely. That's not the way God wants you to respond to your loss.

H. Norman Wright says that forgiveness is a crucial part of the healing process: "If we don't forgive, that means we are carrying resentment and bitterness, which begins to eat away at our body and our mind. Forgiveness is not just for the other person, but it's for us as well, and it is obeying what God has asked us to do."

Losing someone is bad enough, but when you add to that the injustice or carelessness or brutality of someone's actions that resulted in the death, your grief becomes even more complicated and unbearable. The choice to forgive does not mean you condone someone else's actions. It means you are choosing what's best for you and for the people around you whom you care for.

Our goal is to help you respond in a way that is healthy for you, and brings the most glory to God. That means you should forgive. We understand it may be extremely difficult for you to consider forgiving someone, but it's in your best interest to do so. And God will give you the strength to do it.

What Is Forgiveness?

First, let's make sure we understand what forgiveness is by considering one of Jesus's parables.

> The kingdom of heaven is like a king who wanted to settle accounts with his servants. As he began the settlement, a man who owed him ten thousand bags of gold was brought to him. Since he was not able to pay, the master ordered that he and his wife and his children and all that he had be sold to repay the debt.
>
> At this the servant fell on his knees before him. "Be patient with me," he begged, "and I will pay back everything." The servant's master took pity on him, canceled the debt and let him go. (Matt. 18:23–27)

Let's pause the story. Right away, we learn many things about forgiveness. According to Jesus's story, forgiveness means choosing to cancel a debt, to absorb the cost. It is a promise and a commitment not to make the other person pay for what he or she did.

So what exactly are you promising in forgiveness? Tim Lane, counselor, explains:

- Promise 1: you're not going to bring up what happened and dwell on it.
- Promise 2: you're not going to bring it up to other people and gossip about the situation.
- Promise 3: you're not going to bring it up to the person in an inappropriate way to make that person pay for the offense.

It's important to note that the king in Jesus's story forgives the same way God forgives us. Jesus uses this story about a king's forgiveness to show us how (and ultimately why) to do the same. This parable and other Scripture passages on forgiveness show us the following:

- Forgiveness is a choice, not a feeling.
- Forgiveness toward another person doesn't mean you condone what the person did or that you trust the person.
- We should forgive the way God forgives.

But there's more to learn about forgiveness. Jesus's story continues.

> But when that servant [who'd been forgiven by the king] went out, he found one of his fellow servants who owed him a hundred silver coins. He grabbed him and began to choke him. "Pay back what you owe me!" he demanded.
>
> His fellow servant fell to his knees and begged him, "Be patient with me, and I will pay it back."
>
> But he refused. Instead, he went off and had the man thrown into prison until he could pay the debt. When the other servants saw what had happened, they were outraged and went and told their master everything that had happened.
>
> Then the master called the servant in. "You wicked servant," he said, "I canceled all that debt of yours because you begged me to. Shouldn't you have had mercy on your fellow servant just as I had on you?" (Matt. 18:28–33)

The first half of this story helps us see what forgiveness is. The second half shows us why we should do it—no matter how deeply we've been wronged. God wants us to forgive others the same way he's forgiven us. Kay Arthur, Bible teacher and widow, explains, "How can I, who've been forgiven what I have done against a holy and perfect and righteous God, refuse to forgive another?"

If you're struggling to forgive someone, chances are you're giving a lot of thought to what he or she did to cause your loved one's death. This is understandable. After losing someone, it's common to think about the what-ifs and the whys. But focusing on what happened and who did what only makes it more difficult to forgive. It only brings to your mind reasons why you should remain bitter.

Forgiveness Made Easier

Forgiveness becomes easier and makes more sense when, instead of focusing on the wrong done to you, you think about God's character and the manner in which he forgave you. Here are four truths about God that, when considered together, provide a strong reason for you to forgive others.

1. God is perfect and hates sin.
2. In spite of his perfection and hatred of sin, God chose to forgive you for sinning against him.
3. To God, your sin was, as represented in the parable, an enormous debt.
4. God was under no obligation to forgive you, yet he did it freely.

Lorraine Peterson, whose mother was killed as a result of a car accident, explains how thinking about these truths led her to forgive: "As Christ has forgiven you, you're to forgive other people. God is perfect and he forgave me. Who am I to say, 'I'm not going to forgive that other person; he doesn't deserve it.' I didn't deserve to be forgiven by God. That person gets my forgiveness whether or not he deserves it."

Sorting out the emotions of grief is complicated. It's complicated even further when your loved one's death occurred because of someone's negligence or violence. If that's your situation, know that God cares for you and invites you to find comfort in him and in the fact that one day he'll put an end to all suffering. But in the midst of your pain and confusion, remember that it is important for you to forgive. Jesus says, "But if you do not forgive others their sins, your Father will not forgive your sins" (Matt. 6:15).

We forgive because we've been forgiven.

I Thought I Forgave Him Already

One of the most confusing aspects of forgiving someone is figuring out if you've actually done it. For example, today you may decide to forgive someone, but next week you may find yourself being tempted to wish harm on him or her. Did you really forgive?

Look at it this way. Forgiveness isn't a onetime act. You'll have to continue to choose forgiveness whenever you're tempted to hold someone accountable for what he or she has done to you. (That is one difference between the way God forgives and the way we forgive.) Rochelle shares how forgiving the boy who shot her son was a process:

> I made the choice to forgive the boy who shot my son. I found myself having to forgive him in my mind several times. At times I would get really upset with him, and emotions started coming out. I've learned that when the emotion is there, then I still have to work at forgiveness.
>
> It's been almost ten years, and I can now think of this boy and not feel any emotion. I can drive by his house sometimes and say, "Oh! I didn't even look," and I can see I have gotten through the process of forgiving. It's not a onetime "I forgive you" and off you go and you're happy.

Forgiveness: Trusting God for Justice

If you feel your loved one was unjustly taken from you, Jesus's teaching on forgiveness may seem impossible to apply. You may feel like you're betraying your loved one by letting the person responsible off the hook. Hopefully, you now see that's not what is happening. When you forgive, you cease playing God and entrust yourself, the situation, and those responsible to an all-powerful, all-knowing, and righteous judge.

> Sometimes justice occurs here on earth; sometimes it occurs later on. What's important is that we're able to not let the

97

offense that occurred against us or our loved one continue to dominate and control our life. If that occurs, then we live a life of bitterness and resentment, and we're missing out on the blessings of God. This is why Jesus talked about forgiveness. It's a freedom for us to experience God's grace and his blessings.

H. Norman Wright

Years after her son was killed, Joanne was able to forgive. How did she do it? She internalized many of the truths mentioned in this chapter. As she says, "After I came to the Lord, I realized that if he could forgive, I needed to forgive." Colossians 3:13 says, "Forgive as the Lord forgave you."

A Word of Encouragement

Forgiveness isn't easy. But God will give you the strength to do it, and his undeserved love gives you the reason. In forgiveness, we see the kindness of God once again. He has provided a way to escape the destructive consequences of bitterness. Forgiving others also gives us the opportunity to share the kind of love, acceptance, and forgiveness we've undeservedly received from God. While forgiveness may not be the solution you expected, it's God's idea, and therefore it's best. Trust him. He does not lie. Believe that he's right when he says it's better for you to forgive than to hold a grudge.

12

Dealing with Regret
and Guilt

We can always think of the things we did wrong.

Jan

He will also keep you firm to the end, so that you will be
blameless on the day of our Lord Jesus Christ.

1 Corinthians 1:8

Feelings of guilt and regret can complicate your grief.
This chapter will help you discover how to deal with
those troubling thoughts.

You're Plagued by Regrets

I wish I had . . . If only I had . . . If you are focused on how
you might have prevented your loved one's death, it will be
difficult for you to heal.

One way to lessen your feelings of regret is to talk to other people about these feelings. Other people can help put your regrets in perspective for you.

> I laid awake at night thinking, "Oh, Lord, I wish I had taken him to Duke [Hospital]. Why didn't I think about it?" just punishing myself. One thing that helped me was talking to other people. I thought it was my fault because I didn't take him to Duke. But one of my friends told me, "You did all you knew to do." Which is true. That's all I knew to do.
>
> Annie

H. Norman Wright says we should challenge our assumptions about what we should or shouldn't have done to prevent our loved one's death.

> Sometimes we confuse responsibility with accidents. "I *should* have been home." "I *shouldn't* have let him buy that motorcycle." "I *should* have filled the car with gas." Maybe the "shoulds" need to be challenged because in many of the situations you find out there wasn't much you could have done. Even if you had done something, or hadn't done something, it doesn't mean the accident wouldn't have occurred.
>
> H. Norman Wright

Jan, whose teenage son committed suicide, offers two recommendations for dealing with regrets. First, tell yourself the truth about the situation, and, second, focus on the things you did that were right.

First, tell yourself the truth:

> As a parent, the tendency after a suicide is to search your mind from the beginning of your child's life to when it ended, and you think of everything you may have done wrong and said wrong. You can get yourself stuck if you dwell there. You have to come to the place where you realize, "The truth is, I did the best I could with what I knew at the time." And you move on.

Second, consider what you did right. Jan says, "Think about the things you did right. We can always think of the things we did wrong."

When Gracie was overwhelmed by feelings of guilt, she counterattacked those feelings with prayer: "In my mind there was a war going on, and the enemy was trying to make me feel condemned and bad. I began to pray and talk to the Lord about it because it was a tremendous battle."

If your loved one committed suicide, you may wish you'd noticed the signs or that you took your loved one's warnings more seriously. Again, keep in mind that more than likely you did the best you could in the situation.

> Many times when there is a suicide, people will say, "I should have seen it." But with suicide, a person can be so secretive in planning that even a professional would not have picked up on the signs. If somebody wants to take his or her own life, the person will work it so as to be able to do that. But we think we should have intervened in some way. That's a natural feeling, but at some point you have to realize there wasn't anything you could have done.
>
> H. Norman Wright

Another question you may face after a suicide is whether your loved one is in heaven. If your loved one was a Christian, he or she is in heaven. The reason a Christian who commits suicide can still go to heaven is this: the moment a person believes in Christ, God forgives that person of all the sins he or she has committed and will commit. That includes suicide. A believer in Christ does not have to pay the eternal penalty for suicide or any sin committed after being saved.

Another thing that can help you deal with the what-ifs and if onlys is remembering that, ultimately, God determines how long a person lives.

> Your eyes saw my unformed body;
> all the days ordained for me were written in your book
> before one of them came to be. (Ps. 139:16)

Psalm 139:16 clearly states that our life every day is measured, meaning simply that God knows the exact time we will die. He knows when he's going to call us home. There's nothing you can do to extend your life span [or someone else's] one-tenth of a second.

Zig Ziglar

Through a lot of prayer and searching the Scriptures, I realized that God understood my guilt, and I realized that his will would have been accomplished whether I was there for my child or not.

I was afraid of what people were thinking, that I hadn't watched my son closely enough. But there were others there, just several yards away, and I have no idea why they did not hear him or see him. My only conclusion is that his appointed time was up. It took me awhile, through a lot of prayer and the Lord's healing, to finally get rid of the guilt I carried.

Sharon

Do You Need Forgiveness?

Many times your feelings of guilt have nothing to do with sin or wrongdoing. They are mostly false guilt, more like regrets. If you have not done anything wrong, then you do not need forgiveness. "There is true guilt and there is false guilt," explains Jan. "False guilt is from the enemy of our soul. We need to learn to recognize that difference." If you're not clear whether you are dealing with true or false guilt, share your concerns with a few people you trust (a pastor, a counselor, a few close friends). Ask them whether they think your guilt is false or is based on something you need forgiveness for. Getting multiple perspectives on the issue will help you.

There is safety in having many advisers. (Prov. 11:14 NLT)

Dealing with True Guilt

While in many cases you'll discover you are dealing with false guilt, in some situations you may discover you have actually done something wrong. For example, you may have behaved wrongly during the events prior to the death, or you may have acted wrongly toward another person since the death. Maybe it was an unkind word to your now-deceased loved one that you can't take back. Or perhaps you've been particularly cold to family members whom you don't get along with.

It's good to know you are sensitive to the effects your actions have on others. People often rationalize their behavior to the detriment of their spiritual health and relationships. You're to be commended for dealing with this issue honestly. It's likely that you desperately want to let your loved one know you are sorry. To see a way forward in this situation, let's first look at what God thinks about your actions.

Sin Is Serious

As your conscience is telling you, what you've done should be taken seriously. But wallowing in guilt isn't the answer. God has graciously shown us how to deal with our sin so that we can experience forgiveness. Any wrong or sinful act is first and foremost an offense against God. Why? When we sin, *his* rules are broken. If you hold a grudge against someone, in addition to withholding kindness from that person, you're primarily disobeying God's command to show love to everyone.

Another reason sin is so serious is because of its consequences. Romans 6:23 tells us that "the wages of sin is death." This means that the cost, or penalty, of breaking God's rules is eternal separation from God in hell. The severity of the consequence helps us see how offensive sin is to God.

This is where some people's knowledge about God's character trips them up. Because the Bible clearly teaches that God is a loving, caring Father, many assume that if they merely tell God, "I'm sorry," he forgives. When people make that assumption, they're forgetting two things: (1) God is not only loving but also righteous, and (2) the penalty of sin is death—not an apology. If he were to forgive us just because we express sorrow, he'd be breaking his own rule that sin must be punished by death. If he did that, he'd no longer be righteous. Thankfully God has made it possible to forgive and maintain his righteousness.

How to Receive Forgiveness

Instead of condemning everyone for disobeying his laws, God sent his own Son, Jesus, to die on the cross. Jesus willingly paid the penalty of sin and rose from the dead three days later. His death makes it possible for God to forgive justly.

Yet God does not want us to think that Christ's death on the cross provides us with a pass to sin as much as we want to and escape the penalty. As we'll see in the last chapter, God is in the business of renovating the world *and* its inhabitants. He is interested in change. To secure forgiveness, God asks that we

1. admit we are guilty of breaking his commands
2. believe Christ died in our place
3. acknowledge his right to direct our lives

When we do these things, God forgives us of every sin we'll ever commit, or have committed, and gives us the power to live for him. What an amazing offer!

The reason this is such good news is that if you are truly guilty, and you believe Christ died for you, you have been completely forgiven. As the Bible says, "There is now no condemnation for those who are in Christ Jesus" (Rom. 8:1). When Jesus died on the cross, he paid the full penalty for your sins—past, present, and future. Not only did he pay for your sins, but he also lived a perfect life on your behalf. The perfect life Christ lived is credited to you. You're more than forgiven—you are, and always will be, in perfect standing with God!

Now that we understand how God fits into the picture when we talk about forgiveness, we can think more clearly about how to deal with sin you may have committed against your deceased loved one or someone else. What should be clear at this point is the following:

1. If you've done wrong against someone, seeking that person's forgiveness is the right thing to do, but it is also critical that God forgive you for breaking his laws.
2. The only way to experience God's forgiveness is to turn your life over to him, admitting you are a sinner and believing Jesus died in your place to pay the penalty for your sins.
3. Because Jesus lived a perfect life, you have the opportunity to have his perfection credited to you.

If you've never recognized your need for Christ to die in your place to pay for your sins, all you have to do is believe he died for you and agree that God should be the one directing your life. The moment you believe those things, all your sins are forgiven and you are in perfect standing with God.

Being Forgiven by a Deceased Loved One

How does this knowledge help us when it comes to seeking the forgiveness of a deceased loved one? It makes it clear that trying to get closure with your loved one is shortsighted, unless you receive God's forgiveness for what you've done. Also, it helps us understand that regardless of whether the other person would have forgiven you, you can move forward, possibly with some regret, knowing that God accepts you because of Christ's perfect life and sacrificial death.

Unfortunately, at this point, it's impossible to receive forgiveness from your deceased loved one. That opportunity is gone. But if your loved one is in heaven, he or she holds no grudge against you. The Bible teaches that those who are in heaven have been made perfect, so your loved one is not angry with you. Lorraine Peterson shares advice on how to deal with our inability to receive forgiveness from those who've died.

> I suppose everybody has a few regrets when someone very close to you dies: *I wish I had expressed more of my love and concern for that person. I wish I would have taken more time to visit and not have been so busy with my life. Sometimes I really treated this person badly.* Once in a while, the last words I said were in anger.
>
> It's important to realize we cannot go back and we can't redo anything. The best thing to do is to say, "Lord, forgive me," and to accept God's forgiveness and gift of perfect righteousness. I found myself praying after my mom passed away, "Lord, Mom's in heaven, and I wish I could tell her this. Please tell it to her." I don't think that was a wrong prayer, but I also think we should learn something from this to apply to everyday life and that is, How do we treat the people who are still with us?

Seeking Forgiveness from a Friend or Family Member

If you've done wrong to someone who's still alive, you have the opportunity to fix that relationship. First, talk to God and let him know you're aware that what you did was wrong. Thank him for allowing Jesus to die in your place to pay the penalty for that act. Next, go to the person. Admit what you've done, letting the person know you've sinned against that person and God. Then ask him or her to forgive you.

A Word of Encouragement

Feelings of regret are common after the death of a loved one. We encourage you to deal with them in ways that acknowledge your limitations, God's sovereignty over life and death, and his amazing willingness to forgive. Dealing with your feelings won't eliminate all regrets, but it will keep them from haunting you.

13

Anger with God

Anger by its very nature says, "I don't like this."

David Powlison, counselor

In your anger do not sin: Do not let the sun go down while you are still angry.

Ephesians 4:26

This chapter explains how anger with God blocks your healing. As you read, you'll find out how to express your anger in a way that is healthy and how to move from anger to peace.

The Downside of Anger

Every so often prescription drugs are recalled due to potentially dangerous effects. Once thought to be medical breakthroughs, these drugs harmed some people who took them. While initial tests may have revealed successes, long-term use of the drugs proved to be damaging. Anger with God can have the same effect. Initially, being angry with God may make you temporarily feel better, but in the end it doesn't help you heal. Instead, it harms you.

Many who've been through grief will tell you that at some point during their journey they realized they were angry with God. They share moments when, at the height of their pain, they poured out their anger toward God, letting him know exactly how they felt about him taking their loved one. Often people say the experiences were liberating.

These stories are helpful in that they encourage us to be honest with God. A danger of these stories, however, is that they give us the impression that there aren't any negative consequences associated with being angry with God. But there are. For starters, anger with God keeps us from getting to the other side of grief.

Rochelle, whose husband committed suicide and whose son was accidentally shot, shares how anger with God keeps us from healing:

> Once as a little girl I got really angry at my father. He tried to comfort me, and I pushed him away. I went stomping off to my room crying and yelling at my dad, "I hate you. I don't want to talk to you. Leave me alone." As I was sitting in my room crying, I realized nobody was comforting me; nobody was taking care of me. I was in here all by myself crying, and I didn't like that feeling. So I crept back out, and I sneaked up into my daddy's lap and hugged him. He just wrapped his arms around me and loved me through the situation.
>
> It's the same thing with our God. If we get angry with him and shake our fist at him, then we can't receive the comfort he has for us; he can't wrap his arms around us because we are pushing him away.

When we're angry with God, we don't trust him. And when we don't trust him, we don't look to him for comfort.

Unfortunately, this shuts us off from the genuine care God extends. As a result, we end up stuck in grief, and we don't heal.

Shouldn't I Be Angry with God?

How can you be certain God is trustworthy, that his care is genuine? He allowed your loved one to die. Maybe you should be angry?

The reason we know God cares for us is based on an event that took place thousands of years ago. God sacrificed his Son because of his love for people. He allowed his Son to experience unimaginable pain and torture in our place.

God didn't have to do that. We don't deserve his love. The Bible teaches us that while we were God's enemies, he did this for us (Rom. 5:10).

When we grasp the magnitude of his voluntary sacrifice, we realize that no matter how painful our situation is, God's care and concern for us are greater. He gave his Son, whom he loved intensely, to spare us from a hopeless eternity of unimaginable pain and suffering. Therefore, we know God loves us and has our best interest in mind—even if he allows us to experience unimaginable suffering now. In short, God is good, and he proved it at the cross.

Jim and Colleen, who lost their infant child, find great comfort in that fact. As Jim says, "It puts the rest of my life in perspective to go back to God and say, 'Thank you that you would sacrifice your only Son to die for my sins.' "

Colleen agrees. "I want people to know that hope is found in the gospel. God's character is good, and he is the definition of goodness, faithfulness, and truth. When I meditate on his character and on what he's done for me, how can I not say that even though God has a plan I may not understand, he is still good? Hope is found in the finished work of Jesus Christ."

The clearest demonstration of the love of God is the cross. And without a pondering, without an understanding, without a reflection on the meaning of the cross, we're never going to get God's love clear in our mind. We draw the wrong conclusions sometimes.

Larry Crabb, psychologist and Bible teacher

We also shouldn't be angry with God because it puts us in a position we should never assume, that of God's judge. The reason being angry with God is the equivalent of judging him is this: anger with God is the result of an evaluation of his actions. David Powlison explains: "Anger by its very nature says, 'I don't like this, that is wrong, this offends me, that hurts me, I wish this wasn't so.' It has been rightly called the 'moral emotion.' It is the evaluative emotion; it's the emotion that says, 'What is happening does not please me.' "

Telling God You're Angry with Him

At this point, you may feel you have a dilemma. Throughout this book, we've encouraged you to be honest with God about your emotions. Now we're telling you that you shouldn't be angry with him. So what do you do when you're angry with God? Do you tell him or not?

We suggest that you do. But do it humbly. Do it in such a way that you admit you're angry but with an awareness that you have no right to be. You might talk to God about it this way: "God, I don't like what's happened, but I know I shouldn't be angry with you. You love me, and you proved it at the cross. But I still can't understand why you allowed my loved one to die. Help me deal with my feelings in a way that allows me to heal but also pleases you."

If you approach God this way, you can know that he is not displeased or upset with you. How can you be sure? God's acceptance of us as Christians has never been based on our aptitude, behavior, or reaction to loss. God accepts us *only* because of Christ. His death on the cross removed anything that would prevent us from having a relationship with God. In addition, the Bible teaches that no matter how far we fall short, because Christ lived a sinless life for us, God sees us as if we are perfect (Rom. 3:22; 4:24; 2 Cor. 5:21). We enjoy a righteous standing before God. That should give you confidence—confidence to be honest with God about everything because no matter what you tell him, it won't alter what he thinks of you or how much he loves you.

No One Grieves Perfectly

It may be offensive to you to hear that you may need to admit you're wrong for how you feel. We have to remember, however, that the Bible tells us we are all flawed people, and that has implications for our grief. For starters, it means no one will grieve perfectly. You shouldn't presume every reaction you have to your loved one's loss, such as your anger, is productive and God-honoring. You should be aware of negative consequences to your reactions and how to approach God in humility when you make a mistake. But please don't beat yourself up when you do make a mistake.

> I don't think there's a way to do grief perfectly and never make a mistake in how you grieve. I certainly have not done it perfectly in my life. But Christianity is not about doing everything perfectly; it's about letting God show you when you fail and then bringing those failures to him, confessing them, receiving his forgiveness, and moving on. I have seen people grieve with an incredible amount of anger that they're not willing to let the Lord help them with. If you will give your grief to the Lord and say, "Help me handle this," that's the right way to do it. He will help you have a constructive, healing process.
>
> Sue Lutz

It's important to remember that none of us will grieve perfectly. When we remember this, our grief becomes more than a time of healing. It becomes a time of growth. As Paul Tripp says, our grief often reveals things about us that we were not aware of:

> I remember when my dad died, being at the hospital. I was on the elevator by myself, screaming at God. When I got to the bottom, I was shocked at what had come out of me. I had no idea it was there.
>
> Afterward, I sat in my car and I asked for God's forgiveness, and I said, "I know I've been thinking this about you for a long time." God used that moment to expose it.
>
> Grief exposes that what I sing about on Sunday is not always what I believe on Tuesday, when I've gotten the call that a loved one has passed away. Grief exposes that, and that's a good thing.

Moving from Anger to Trust

As you humbly take your anger to God, we hope in time you're able to get to the point where your confusion gives way to trust. Sharon shares how she made this transition:

> I felt like I had been fighting with the Lord. There was warfare in my soul between Satan telling me to hold on to my grief and bitterness, and God telling me to let it go. I went to my son's bedroom, and I cried and pleaded with the Lord.
>
> But I needed peace, and I knew I had to submit to the Lord for peace to happen. At that moment I said, "Lord, instead of saying to you, 'Why did you take my child? Why did you let this happen to me?' I'm saying, 'Okay, Lord, you brought me to this point in my life. What do you have for me to do next?'" I was willing at that point to let God work through me to help others, and that's when the total healing process started—when I was able to let go of my anger, my guilt, and my self-will and to say, "God, take control. You have

a purpose for everything. I'm willing to let you work good through this tragedy."

A Word of Encouragement

As Christians, we shouldn't fear discovering our flaws and shortcomings. God accepts us not on the basis of our good behavior but because of the perfect life Christ lived and his death for our sins. So if you realize you're angry with God, don't be discouraged. It doesn't change how much God loves you.

When God points out areas in which you need to change, he is reaching out to you in love. In this case, he's gently showing you how your anger toward him isn't warranted and that it prevents you from healing. Thank him that he wants you to be honest with him, never pretending you're not angry. Also thank him that he encourages you to communicate with him about what you feel in a way that will help you heal.

Isn't it wonderful to be comforted by a God who is so aware of your weaknesses and gives you so much help and mercy?

14

What Grief Teaches Us

God will take us where we do not want to go in order to produce in us what we could not achieve on our own.

Paul Tripp

It is better to go to a house of mourning
than to go to a house of feasting,
for death is the destiny of everyone;
the living should take this to heart.

Ecclesiastes 7:2

Depending on where you are in the grief process, you may not be ready to think about what you can learn as a result of your grief. Grief is a teacher (a tough one!), and the lessons are difficult. But it is worthwhile to take the lessons with you through the rest of your life. When you are ready, prayerfully consider these important lessons learned through grief.

God Uses Suffering to Help Us Grow

You may be in a place right now where you are so debilitated by grief that you are focusing more on surviving from day to day than on personal growth. But you can still grow and move forward. "The fact is," says Roger, who lost his daughter, "in life we're all going to have sorrow. The question is whether we're going to waste our sorrows or not. Are they going to make us bitter or are they going to make us better?"

"I can look back on my widowhood," shares Elisabeth Elliot, missionary, "and realize there have been priceless lessons I couldn't have learned any other way. I have made steps in the spiritual life that I could not have made if I had refused to accept what God had ordained."

Ecclesiastes 7:4 tells us, "The heart of the wise is in the house of mourning, but the heart of fools is in the house of pleasure." That means there is much to be learned from thinking about death.

Joy and Pain Can Coexist

When you're going through grief, the pain is intense. It affects you emotionally, spiritually, and physically. Wanting it to go away is natural. But we get into trouble when we move from wanting the pain to go away to defining "healing" as the absence of pain. The former is understandable; the latter is impossible. As Lois Rabey says, "Life this side of heaven is full of pain."

That's why defining "healing" as the absence of pain is a trap. God never promised us that this life would be pain-free. You'll always feel a sense of loss when you think about your loved one. It won't be as strong as it is right now, but it will still sting. So how do we heal if we'll always hurt? Lois Rabey, who lost her husband, says we need to realize that joy and pain can coexist.

When I recognized that my pain was going to exist, and that joy can exist in the midst of that, I needed to focus on what that looked like. An incident that really illustrated this for me was when my younger daughter got married. It was a beautiful day. My daughter was posed for the photographer with her flowers, all dressed and ready for the wedding, and all of a sudden she broke her pose and started to cry.

Just at that point her uncle, her dad's brother, came into view. He came up and hugged her, and tears were running down his face, and they didn't say a word to each other. They just held each other, crying, and then he backed up and wiped away her tears and gave her a thumbs-up and went on. And all of us watching knew on this very positive day, in a beautiful setting with everybody completely happy, that there was an acknowledgment of the pain that her father/his brother was not there. That became my image of what peace and pain living together looks like.

Understanding that joy and pain can coexist can help you see how people can be joyful after suffering devastating losses. For instance, knowing the depth of your own pain, you may be tempted to think, *That person is faking it; there is no way she could be happy.* While some people *are* faking it, or repressing their feelings, there are those who are genuinely joyful—despite the fact they are hurting deeply. The final chapter of this book explains why this is possible.

Time Doesn't Heal All Wounds

A common misconception is that time is the healer of wounds. But if a person does not deal with the source of pain, that person is not going to heal, regardless of how much time passes.

God is the source of healing, but God isn't a magic wand. He wants to help you face and sort through your hurts and emotions. You need to seek his counsel and obey his Word day by day until you finally come to the place of true healing. The amount of time it takes depends on your background, coping skills, past experiences with loss and grief, support system, commitment level to doing the hard work of grief, spiritual maturity, and more.

You Harvest What You Sow

You've heard it said, "You reap what you sow." When you grieve, you see just how true that statement is. The daily choices you make about how you grieve, what you think and say, what you do with your time, how you relate with people are what you are sowing, what you are planting in your life. Whatever you plant will be what grows and comes out of you.
Paul Tripp says:

> Maybe I'm eight months into a grief experience, and I'm harvesting loneliness. What I realize as I look at that harvest is I'm not stuck in loneliness; rather, I blew off the people in my life. I told them they didn't understand. I didn't return phone calls. I didn't answer emails.
>
> This is my harvest. Rather than saying, "I'm trapped in loneliness," I decide to plant new seeds. I'm going to go back to that person and say, "You tried to help me, and I was pretty hard on you. I need you in my life. Please forgive me and call me." What will happen is those seeds will grow into a new harvest.

Life Was Always out of Control, but God Is Sovereign (in Control)

Our ability to plan is an obvious blessing. Unfortunately, we can dupe ourselves into thinking that our ability to plan means we are in control. Losing a loved one makes us painfully aware that we're not.

> Before the death, all we're thinking about is, "I need to pick up the dry cleaning. What am I going to make for dinner? Whom should we get together with this weekend?" It feels

like control, but when we lose somebody, we bump into the reality that we're not God—we don't have control.

Sue Lutz

Even though life is out of *your* control, it doesn't mean it's out of control. In the Bible, God tells us that he controls everything. In other words, he is sovereign.

> Remember the former things, those of long ago;
> I am God, and there is no other;
> I am God, and there is none like me.
> I make known the end from the beginning,
> from ancient times, what is still to come.
> I say, "My purpose will stand,
> and I will do all that I please." . . .
> What I have said, that will I bring about;
> what I have planned, that will I do. (Isa. 46:9–11)

God Takes No Pleasure in Your Loved One's Death

Reading verses like Isaiah 46:9–11 can be troubling, particularly if your loved one died violently or unexpectedly. You may wonder, *Did God* want *this to happen?* No, not in the sense that he took pleasure in your loved one's death. God is a loving Father who weeps over sin, death, and suffering. The Bible also reveals that God is a righteous judge who will punish all wrongdoing associated with one person taking another's life. So while God is in control, he is not culpable. An example of this is found in the way the apostle Peter shares the factors behind the plot to kill Jesus.

> [Jesus] was handed over to you by God's deliberate plan and foreknowledge; and you, with the help of wicked men, put him to death by nailing him to the cross. (Acts 2:23)

In this verse, Peter makes it clear that Christ's death was part of God's plan, but those who put him to death were responsible for their actions. While difficult to comprehend, this passage provides a framework for understanding how God maintains his sovereignty without being responsible for a loved one's death. Everything that happens, including the death of a loved one, is somehow part of his sovereign plan, even though we may never fully understand how or why. But this confusing truth can also be a basis for hope.

> It's difficult, exciting, and scary to deal with the question, "What does God have to do with my grief and suffering?" It seems like it would be nice to be able to say "nothing," but think about the logic of that. If God has no contact whatsoever with my suffering, if he has no control over it, then he is positively unable to help me in it.
>
> The Bible says in Psalm 46 that God is our refuge and strength, an ever-present help in times of trouble, not an ever-present help *after* times of trouble. God is ruling his world and is in control of my life, and that includes my suffering.
>
> Paul Tripp

Resetting Your Expectations

One thing that can keep us from coming to terms with God's sovereignty is that we expect something different from what God has promised. We have to remember that God's assertion of his sovereignty is not a pledge to explain his plans to us in detail. If your prerequisite for accepting God's sovereignty is understanding his plan, you'll never move forward in your healing from grief. What's worse, you're setting yourself up to be frustrated with God. You're demanding that God do something he said he would not. In fact, he tells us that even if he tried to explain himself, we couldn't understand. That's why the Bible says, "Have you ever come on anything quite like this extravagant generosity of God, *this deep, deep wisdom? It's way over our heads. We'll never figure it out*" (Rom. 11:33 Message, emphasis added).

119

The Benefit of Trusting in God's Sovereignty

Why is it so important that we understand God is in control? When life feels out of control, understanding God's sovereignty keeps us from concluding that our suffering is the result of an impersonal force like karma, the result of chaos, or evidence that God does not exist. A loving, caring God is in control of everything that happens to us, and it's all been a part of his plan from the beginning.

> To trust in the sovereignty of God is not just accepting that God is in control of the universe around us; it is acknowledging his control of our lives. It is to say to God, "I'm yours. You can do anything you want with me." Because we know God is good, and that he has our best interests in his heart and mind, we can entrust ourselves and those we love to him: "But I trust in you, LORD; I say, 'You are my God.' My times are in your hands" (Ps. 31:14–15).
>
> Knowing God is sovereign doesn't exempt us from grief. In reality, the sovereignty of God is a hard truth to accept because if he is in control of everything, we wonder why he has allowed this universe to be ordered in a way that causes us such pain. But without confidence in God's sovereignty, life becomes meaningless, hope for justice fades, and everything seems random.
>
> Nancy Guthrie

We hope you'll see that while God's sovereignty can be difficult to accept, it is also what you can hold on to when you don't understand, when your loss seems senseless and unbearable, and when the future seems uncertain.

God Uses Suffering for Good

We mentioned that God hasn't promised to explain every detail of why he's allowing your life to unfold the way it is. But that doesn't mean God will not share any of his plan with you. In fact, he reveals a great deal.

One of the most eye-opening and instructive aspects of his plan is laid out for us in Romans 8.

> And we know that in all things God works for the good of those who love him, who have been called according to his purpose. For those God foreknew he also predestined to be conformed to the image of his Son. (vv. 28–29)

These verses are remarkable. They tell us God uses all things that occur in the life of a Christian to bring about something good. This does not mean God wants you to consider your loved one's death a good event. Nor does it mean God thinks your loved one's death was a good thing. Instead, he wants us to understand that he will take your loved one's death and bring about something good from it.

You may find this difficult to believe in light of the suffering you've been going through. The difficulty in grasping this truth often lies in our personal definition of what "good" is. If we define "good" as God always giving us what we want or doing what we think is best, then we will conclude that Romans 8:28 and 29 are lies. But Romans 8:29 tells us that the good God speaks of is us becoming more like Christ. Edward Welch explains why this verse may be difficult for you to accept and what to do to get to the point where it becomes meaningful to you:

> People who have gone through bereavement have probably heard Romans 8:28 before, and they've hated it: "And we know that in all things God works for the good of those who love him, who have been called according to his purpose." Well, it doesn't feel good, and it doesn't feel like something to be thankful for. Romans 8:29 explains the passage a little bit more. It tells us what the good is. The "good" is we are going to be looking more and more like Jesus Christ.
> Now here's the problem for me: there are times in the midst of suffering where the only good I can imagine would be the alleviation of my suffering, the resurrection of the one I lost.

But apparently there is an even greater good. That somehow the Spirit of the living God is going to make me look more and more like the person I was intended to be. I am going to look more and more like Christ.

What I need is the body of Christ in the midst of my bereavement to remind me, to help me to believe, that that is good. And I've asked people to pray for me in the midst of hardship: "Could you pray that I would truly believe that being conformed to the image of Jesus Christ is the greatest thing in life?"

A Word of Encouragement

We hope you'll spend time thinking about the lessons in this chapter. It may take time for you to grasp some of them. But that's okay. God will open your eyes to understand them if you ask him to help you do so. And as you grieve with hope, you'll probably learn many other lessons that are precious to you. Ask God to allow you to use them someday to comfort someone else who is grieving.

15

How Do I Get through This?

You will find peace only through surrender.

Sharon

Then I said, "Here I am. . . . I have come to do your will, my God."

Hebrews 10:7

Moving forward in healing and hope involves surrendering. "Surrendering what?" you may ask. This chapter explains how surrender can be a good thing and what you'll need to surrender in order to get through grief.

Getting through Grief Involves Surrendering

Let's say you are running late for a flight. You rush to check in your bags, only to find out there's no room for your luggage on the plane. The airline representative suggests placing your bags on a different flight to the same place. While inconvenient, you will likely surrender your bags because you want to get to your destination.

The same is true in grief. If you're going to "take flight" or move forward in your healing, you need to (permanently) surrender some things. But we're not talking about luggage. We're talking about anything you're holding on to that conflicts with God's plan for your healing.

The things that conflict with God's plan for your healing are certain ideas, beliefs, and coping strategies. It can be difficult to identify these things in your life much less surrender them. We interviewed many people who've gone through grief, and we discovered some key things you'll need to surrender to move forward.

You may not have thought of surrendering as a key for getting through grief. In fact, when you think of the word *surrender*, you may not think of it as a good thing at all. "We will never surrender!" is the war cry. But what if the beliefs, standards, or ways of living you are holding so tightly are wrong? What if they are ultimately bringing you harm? What if they are severely limiting your effectiveness and potential? You might then change your war cry and see that the stronger, wiser choice is to surrender those wrong ideas and adopt new ones.

Surrender means to yield control or power to someone or something else; it means to give up something in favor of another choice. Surrender enables you to let go of things you are holding too tightly and to accept an even better option. Surrender frees you to be able to hope again.

Things You Need to Surrender

Your Plans and Dreams

Nancy, whose daughter died, shares, "From the day the doctors told us our daughter Hope would have only a few months to live, I began letting go of my dreams for her and for myself. Every surrendered dream brought a new wave of pain." Death shatters many of the hopes, dreams, and plans you had for your loved one and for you in relation to your loved one. If you are grieving the loss of your hopes and dreams, it's okay; you're not alone.

> When my daughter died, our dream had shattered that she was going to grow up to be a godly woman. She wasn't even going to grow up. All this love we'd invested, all this time to teach her about the Lord and to help her memorize Scripture, it just seemed like it was all in vain.
>
> Roger

> I felt like I had been cheated because my husband had just retired and I felt like we could have a little life to ourselves for a while. But evidently he didn't see it that way.
>
> Katie, whose husband committed suicide

While it's normal to grieve the loss of your plans and dreams, if you hold on to them and refuse to surrender them, you'll soon find yourself stuck in grief. Your refusal to let go likely means you don't find God trustworthy. And since your relationship with him is vital to your healing, this isn't a good place to be.

The key to surrendering your plans, hopes, and dreams to the Lord is realizing that he is God and that he has a plan for you. Jeremiah 29:11 summarizes God's intentions toward you, no matter how bad things are for you: " 'For I know the plans I have for you,' declares the LORD, 'plans to prosper you and not to harm you, plans to give you hope and a future.' "

Your Expectations That Your Faith Should Have Shielded the Pain

Some people expected that their faith in God would insulate them from feeling the pain of grief or at least make it go away quicker. As David Guthrie, who lost two of his children, said, "I think I expected our faith would make this hurt less, but it didn't."

That's not how faith works. If you think God is supposed to keep you from feeling pain, you're mistaken. Faith in God doesn't guarantee good feelings. It sustains us in their absence. Edward Welch explains, "Faith, true faith, is expressed in the shadows, in this valley of the shadow of death when we can't see our God clearly and we say, 'Lord, help me to trust you because the loss still feels like it's going to overwhelm me.'"

If you've been praying to God to take the pain away and it hasn't lifted, it does not mean he's not listening to you or that your faith is necessarily weak. More than likely it points to the fact that you loved the person who died and that his or her death created multiple losses for you to grieve. Sometimes it takes time to realize just how much you've lost. That's one of many reasons grief can last so long.

Your Demand for Answers

We have commended you for taking your questions to God. In doing so, you demonstrate that you believe he has all the answers—which he does. However, demanding that God give you specific answers to your questions will have negative consequences. Larry Crabb says that demanding answers will "turn you into a closet atheist or a very angry Christian." He adds, "There's not a lot of difference between the two," because if you're in one of those categories, you won't seek God for advice on how to heal. To be able to accept fully the healing God offers, you need to surrender your demand for answers.

One of the reasons that demanding answers from God leaves us frustrated is that the Bible tells us there are certain things God has chosen not to share with us. "Some things we are never going to understand," says Barbara Johnson. "I don't understand why two beautiful Christian boys, whom I raised right, who loved the Lord, were taken at such an early age. But that's why I claim Deuteronomy 29:29: 'The secret things belong to the Lord.' There are secret things that are going to happen to us, and we're never going to understand them this side of heaven. We're not going to have all the answers." If you believe that healing from grief depends on you getting ultimate answers from God, you'll never heal because you'll never get the answers you're looking for.

Another reason to surrender your demand for answers to certain questions is because it's keeping you from listening to the answers God *is* giving you. Deuteronomy 29:29 continues by saying, "But the things revealed belong to us and to our children forever, that we may follow all the words of this law." This verse tells us that although God will not reveal everything to us, there are many things he wants to share with us: promises, truths, and ideas that empower and encourage us to obey him and experience blessings. God wants to talk to you. He wants to tell you how to heal from your grief.

Here's something you can do instead of repeatedly asking the same questions of God. Ask different questions. Are there questions you can ask that would move you forward in a way that's healthy, that would draw you to healing instead of making your grief worse? Are there questions that will help not only you but also those around you?

God wants you to ask him questions. Keep that dialogue going! But also consider where your questions are leading you. Do they guide you toward a closer understanding of who God is and a greater dependence on him? Or are they leading you in a different direction?

Tim Clinton, president of the American Association of Christian Counselors, says, "The best way to understand healthy grief is to see people who move from the 'Why, God; it's so wrong; it's so unfair; why now and why me?' to a 'how' statement. 'How, God, do I go on? How do I get what I need day by day so I can put one foot in front of the other and allow the emotions to come as necessary?'"

Other questions you can ask of God are:

- How am I to deal with this?
- How can I honor both you and my loved one right now?
- What can I learn through this experience?
- How do you want me to function and grow from this point on?

Surrendering your demand for answers involves ceasing those demands, ending the constant drive to figure out why, and understanding that the better, more productive choice involves discovering what God wants to share with you.

Your Demand to Feel Better Right Away

If you expect or demand that your pain be lifted quickly, you may get frustrated with God and conclude that seeking him isn't helpful. Once again, you are making demands of God that are not helping you, that aren't in your own best interest, and that are based on feelings.

Ecclesiastes reminds us that just as there is a time to be happy, there is also a time to grieve. This is your season of grief. Don't rush it or demand to see its conclusion; instead, surrender this demand to God.

Your grief process is God's way of allowing you to come to terms with the significance of your loss and giving you time to heal. As Pastor Norman Peart says, you can also see your journey through grief as a way of honoring your loved one:

> It is very hard to think that grief is going to be a fast process. It's a sign of the love that we truly felt for our loved one; and therefore, a deep love is going to hurt even more when a deep love is lost. We should honor individuals that way. We need to also realize that because of the deepness of that love, it will take more time to work through it. It may take months, and it may take years.

When you surrender your demand to feel better now, you are accepting the assignment to wait. While waiting for healing, instead of focusing on the pain, you can shift your focus to what God is doing in you as you grieve. James 1 teaches that one of God's purposes in taking us through difficult situations is to transform us. He knows your deepest needs, and he knows your greatest potential: "Consider it pure joy, my brothers and sisters, whenever you face trials of many kinds, because you know that the testing of your faith develops perseverance. Let perseverance finish its work so that you may be mature and complete, not lacking anything" (James 1:2–4). This passage does not tell you to consider the death of your loved one to be pure joy. Rather, you can find joy in the fact that God is going to use this terrible situation to help you mature spiritually. That is a source of great joy.

Another reason we need to surrender our desire to heal immediately is that if we don't, we amplify our suffering. In addition to grieving our loss, we are also dealing with the disappointing perception that God is letting us down by allowing us to experience such deep pain.

We have to realize that certain promises are for today and some very different and distinct promises God gives us later. That means we don't demand heaven (no suffering, no pain, no death) now. Instead, we wait, focusing on and being thankful for what God is doing in us.

Your Dependence

We discussed earlier in the book the benefits of surrendering your independence and accepting help from other people and God. In surrendering your independence, you are showing that you understand you cannot heal through your own strength and efforts; you cannot heal alone.

Here we focus on the need to surrender your dependence on anything other than God to help you heal. It's important to recognize that while other people, nature, new hobbies, support groups, counselors, volunteer work, etc., are helpful in healing, these are gifts from God. They are not to be depended on in and of themselves.

You also need to let go of anything you are dependent on that God would not want you to use to find comfort. Such things include drugs, alcohol, food, shopping, pornography, and sex. These things don't help you heal; in fact, they complicate your grief by adding other issues to your life that you have to deal with. Jeremiah 2:13 says, "My people have committed two sins: They have forsaken me, the spring of living water, and have dug their own cisterns, broken cisterns that cannot hold water." Larry Crabb explains, "God looked down on his people and said, 'You people are really foolish. Here you're thirsty, which is fine. I made you thirsty, and I'm full of water. Yet you walk right by me, the spring of living water, to dig for yourselves [to try to take control of the healing *your* way] broken cisterns that can hold no water.'"

God alone offers true healing when you surrender to him your dependence on things that don't truly satisfy:

> Come, all you who are thirsty,
>   come to the waters;
> and you who have no money,
>   come, buy and eat!
> Come, buy wine and milk
>   without money and without cost.
> Why spend money on what is not bread,
>   and your labor on what does not satisfy?
> Listen, listen to me, and eat what is good,
>   and you will delight in the richest of fare.
> (Isa. 55:1–2)

Talk to your pastor or a Christian counselor and let him or her know what you've been using to numb your pain. Also ask for help in learning how to satisfy your soul with the food that God offers.

A Word of Encouragement

Throughout the grief process, you will discover ideas, plans, and ways of coping that will not help you heal. Pray that God will give you the willingness and the faith to surrender them to him and to trust that his ways are better for you, even though you may not fully understand why or how.

Sharon, who lost her son and miscarried two babies, says, "I just want to say to anybody who is struggling, 'Now is the time to surrender to God's will because you will find peace only through surrender.'"

16

Grieving with Hope and Joy

We're going to have tough days, but that's all right because the big day is yet to come.

Joseph Stowell

Brothers and sisters, we do not want you to . . . grieve like the rest of mankind, who have no hope.

1 Thessalonians 4:13

You can have hope and joy amid your suffering and sorrow. This chapter explains how this is possible and the necessity of discovering hope and joy in order to remain on the path of true healing.

Hope and Joy Are Possible

As you emerge from the sorrow of losing your loved one, you'll begin to look forward again. When you do, you'll see things with a new set of eyes. You'll see the world for what it is—a scary, temporary place. You'll realize that any time you visit the doctor, he may inform you that your body has turned against you. You'll know that before you're ready, enjoyable moments with loved ones will become bittersweet memories. At times you'll want to scream, as it seems people are conspiring to stay busy in an attempt to distract themselves from the fact that we all die.

This awareness can cause you to ask, "How does God expect me to have hope and joy in the midst of a world filled with pain and suffering?"

It's important that you find the right answers to that question. If you don't, you'll become cynical about what God has to say, distancing yourself from him and his people. After that, you're likely to join the conspiracy of busyness, engaging in new relationships, hobbies, and so on to distract yourself from hurt and inevitable death.

Pushing away from God, or distracting yourself with busyness, is not a good way to respond to the realities that death awakens you to. For one, it puts you on a carousel of despair, going around and around, emotionally up and down, as you move from one moment to the next. Also, it prevents you from glorifying God in the midst of your suffering as you become increasingly self-centered, constantly seeking new (but ineffective) ways to escape the pain. Finally, the last thing you want to do is try to survive this scary, temporary world without God's help.

There is an alternative. You can have hope and joy in the midst of this world. You can have joy because of what God has already done for you, and you can have hope because of what he's promised to do.

God Has a Plan to Fix the World

God isn't blind. When he tells us to have hope, he's fully aware that he's asking us to do this in a world that has its share of problems. But God wants us to know he's promised to fix it. In fact, he's already begun. When we focus on that, and personally get on board with God's plan to fix the world, hope is a natural result. Here's why.

The Bible teaches us that God sent Jesus to carry out a plan to end all suffering. Because of what Jesus came to do, the Bible tells us that one day there will be no more tears.

> Then I saw "a new heaven and a new earth." . . . I heard a loud voice from the throne saying, ". . . There will be no more death or mourning or crying or pain, for the old order of things has passed away." He who was seated on the throne said, "I am making everything new!" (Rev. 21:1, 3–5)

One day there will be no more disease, no more tragedy, no more suffering—no more death. That's a reason for hope and celebration! But it gets better.

God is going to do more than stop death, disease, famines, and natural disasters; he's also going to renew people. We all need to be renewed. Why? Because the thing that causes all the world's problems is the same thing that causes us to be selfish, bitter, unforgiving, angry, and unreasonable. The Bible calls it sin. The Bible also teaches us that sin affects everything: our thinking, our relationships, our environment, and our health.

In addition to making the world a difficult place to live, your sin is a barrier to having a relationship with God. Your sin also prevents you from experiencing the comfort and healing he offers you. But Jesus came to offer a way to remove that barrier. Here's how he did it.

Jesus lived a perfect life, and then he died. Because God says sin is such a serious offense to him that it must be punished by eternal separation from God, Jesus paid the debt for our sins by dying on the cross as an offering to God. Since he was not just a man but also one with God, he rose from the dead three days later. This was the only way to defeat sin and death and to pave the way for the tear-free world God has promised.

But having knowledge of what Jesus came to do is not enough to experience the benefits of it, nor is it a reason for hope.

God's Plan to Fix the World Gets Personal

One of the keys to hope is personally getting on board with God's plan to fix the world. That's because the gifts of forgiveness and the promise of eternity with God in a perfect, tear-free reality become yours only as you admit that you too need to be fixed—and trust Christ to do it for you. It's the key to experiencing lasting joy, and it lays a foundation for hope. If you've never done this before, here's all you have to do:

1. Admit you have sinned. (This means you've acted in ways and have had attitudes that do not please God.)
2. Believe that Jesus died in your place to pay your sin debt.

That's all there is to it. If you believe those things, the sin barrier is gone. You have a relationship with God. He accepts you because of what Christ did for you, not because of anything you've done or will do. As the Bible says:

> He saved us, not because of righteous things we had done, but because of his mercy. (Titus 3:5)

> For it is by grace you have been saved, through faith—and this is not from yourselves, it is the gift of God—not by works, so that no one can boast. (Eph. 2:8–9)

You Can Have Joy Because of What Christ Has Done for You

Imagine that New York City's top chef was coming to your home for dinner. You would want the meal to be perfect. You'd be nervous about his judgment, yet you'd know the whole time you could never meet his level of excellence. God is perfect, and you may be fearful about how he'll judge you. We can never meet his level of excellence by our own efforts. Thankfully, Christ has already met God's requirement of perfection for us. Jesus lived a perfect life on our behalf. All the words he said, the choices he made, and his thoughts, actions, and motivations were sinless. Because Jesus lived this way for us, and God judges us based on what Jesus did, we can have great joy and relief. Although we're not perfect, we can have Christ's righteousness.

We can also have great joy when we think of how God has spared us from unimaginable suffering. As the Scriptures say, "It is a fearful thing to fall into the hands of the living God" (Heb. 10:31). But because of what Christ has done for us, we've been spared that! As the Bible says, "Blessed are they whose transgressions are forgiven, whose sins are covered" (Rom. 4:7).

We do not mean to trivialize your grief experience, but no matter how devastating or prolonged your grief is, the pain and suffering it brings could never compare to the pain and suffering of paying your sin debt. Doing so would be far worse than any pain you could experience on earth. In the midst of our grief, we can always comfort ourselves with this fact. God has gone to great lengths (sending his beloved Son to die) to spare us from the worst suffering imaginable.

Having joy, however, does not mean that during your grief you should always have a smile on your face or that when asked, "How are you doing?" you respond, "Praise the Lord, I'm not going to hell!" It simply means that even on the darkest day of your journey of grief, you can look back to the cross and remind yourself that God is unquestionably for you.

You Can Have Hope Because of What Christ Will Do for You

While we find joy in reflecting on the meaning of Christ's death, we also have hope because we know God is not satisfied with the way things are and he already has a plan in motion to change the world. Thankfully, life will not always be the way it is now. And if you have a relationship with Christ, you'll be able to experience the anticipation of a brand-new, tear-free world.

Here are just a few of the things Christ will provide for us in the new heaven and new earth.

A Safe and Stable Place

Life in this world is not safe or stable. Bad things happen. People let us down. Danger can feasibly lurk around every corner. No matter how hard we try to protect ourselves and our loved ones, we can't always do it.

"Heaven is safe," declares Christian speaker Anne Graham Lotz. "When you're inside those walls, nothing can hurt you; nothing can come in and harm you. Heaven is described as a place that has twelve foundations, and each foundation has a different layer of a semi-precious stone. Heaven is a stable place. There's an instability to life, and we can't be absolutely sure of today or tomorrow. But heaven doesn't change. It's absolutely solid. You can stand on it and know it's not going to sway underneath you."

A Place You Can See Your Loved Ones

How wonderful it will be to see our loved ones again. For our loved ones in heaven, time is not an issue; for us, we are limited to the boundaries of time, and we will have to wait. How comforting and exciting to look forward to this reunion day!

When Zig and Jean Ziglar's daughter Suzan died, instead of wallowing in self-pity, the Ziglars focused on the fact that she was in heaven. Zig remembers the Lord encouraging him to do so. "God speaks to me mostly in the Bible, but this time I got the strong impression that God was saying to me, 'I want to assure you that Suzan is with me. She's in my hands. She is fine.'"

The Ziglars experienced great comfort knowing Suzan was in heaven. Zig shares, "Not too long after Suzan died, we were in Washington for an event. One morning we had slept a little late, and as we were walking toward the elevator, I blurted out, 'I wonder where Suzan is and what she's doing.' Then it hit me like a ton of bricks. I knew exactly where she was and what she was doing. That was one of those epiphany moments."

A *Life Lived Forever with Jesus*

The most wonderful thing about heaven is that Jesus will be there. We may struggle with the idea that seeing Jesus will be better than seeing our lost loved one, but it is true. The glory of being in the presence of the Lord will cause us to put all our relationships in the proper perspective. In heaven we will understand, more than ever, that God is the hub, the source of all things good and right and lovely. We will rejoice in his amazing goodness, and through him we will enjoy our wonderful reunions. "Make no mistake about it: the thing that makes heaven heaven is the fact that God is there," says Anne Graham Lotz.

Joni Eareckson Tada, founder of Joni and Friends Ministries, explains further:

> When we get to heaven, our discovery of God is going to be an eternal adventure because we'll be like children—constantly discovering, constantly at wonder, constantly amazed. When we get to heaven, we'll see some facet of God that will simply blow us away, and like the seraphim we'll say, "Holy, Holy, Holy, Lord God Almighty."
>
> And when we pause to stop and contemplate that, as the seraphim no doubt do when they cover their faces with their wings, the next time we look up, God has turned over some other marvelous facet about him and it's "Whoa! Holy, Holy, Holy, I never knew that about you, God. How marvelous!" This constant building and flowing of joy, this effervescing discovery about our eternal Father will go on for infinity.

Our experience in heaven won't be static or inert. It will be active. It will be dynamic.

It's comforting to think about heaven, knowing your loved one is safe, secure, and completely happy. The late Bill Bright, founder of Campus Crusade for Christ, shared, "The split second we cease to breathe here on planet earth, we begin to breathe celestial air, and we have no reason to grieve. Several of my family members are now with our Lord, and I don't grieve over that because they're better off than I am. I miss them, but I would never want them to come back to planet earth. Their abode in heaven is incredibly greater in meaning and fulfillment than this place could ever provide."

He continued, "One day the newspaper will say 'Bill Bright is now with the Lord,' but don't shed tears of grief, shed tears of joy if you wish, because I'm far better off in the presence of the King of Kings and the Lord of Lords, my wonderful Savior, than I could ever be here on earth."

I know my daughter is in heaven and she's safe. I know I'm going to see my child again. The Bible promises me that. And I know if she had her choice, she wouldn't come back down here.

Ann

Heaven is a perfect place. There's no sadness, no pain, no anger, no unforgiveness. It gives me comfort to know my son will never have to feel pain. He'll never know the depths of despair. He's protected from that in heaven. It comforts me to know that he is with the Lord because what greater reward at the end of your life than to be with him.

Joanne

Is My Loved One in Heaven?

While the new reality that God creates will be a stunning place, you may be concerned your loved one won't experience it. Worrying about that can keep you in deep despair. But your loved one may have become a Christian without you knowing it. Simply coming to God in faith, believing Christ died on the cross for you, saves you from sin. You don't have to pray a certain prayer, be baptized, or join a church. All it takes is placing your faith in Christ alone to save you from your sin. In some cases, you don't know for sure what your loved one believed before he or she died.

> As a pastor I've stood next to people whose loved ones had died who weren't sure whether their loved one had ever come to know Christ as personal Savior. The most important thing to remember is that God is fair and just and wise and loving. Whatever he does with my loved one will be fair and just and wise and loving. God cannot deny himself. We do not know what our loved ones did in that last flickering moment of life in the quietness of their soul.
>
> Joseph Stowell

The Benefit of Anticipating What God Will Do

Eagerly anticipating what God has promised prevents us from placing our hope in things that have the potential to disappoint. This does not mean we stop enjoying relationships, events, nature, etc. It means we enjoy them as gifts from God without depending on them to be sources of joy, happiness, or security.

We see this principle applied when the apostle Paul tells his protégé how to instruct those who are rich. He says, "Command those who are rich in this present world not to be arrogant nor to put their hope in wealth, which is so uncertain, but to put their hope in God, who richly provides us with everything for our enjoyment" (1 Tim. 6:17). Paul does not downplay the pleasure that comes from money or the fact that God gives us money (and all other things) for us to enjoy. But he says our hope should not be in money because it is uncertain. Our hope should be in God.

We fix our eyes not on what is seen, but on what is unseen, since what is seen is temporary, but what is unseen is eternal. (2 Cor. 4:18)

A Firm Reason for Hope

What Christ has done for us on the cross and what God promises he will do are the basis for hope and joy in this imperfect world. God has dealt with the source of the world's problems—sin. One day we will be with him in a world clear of all present dangers.

Since our hope is rooted in a God whose plans cannot be frustrated and who has demonstrated his power over death, our hope is more than wishful thinking.

> I've watched a lot of girls grow up, and after they go to their first wedding with their family, they wonder, *I wonder if I'll get a day like this?* It's a hope; it's a wish; it's a maybe. But then one day along comes this valiant knight in shining armor, sweeps her off her feet, throws her over the steed, whispers in her ear "June fourth," and drops the rock on her finger. Now something critical has happened. There's been a transition from the "hope so" kind of hope to an attachment to a certain future reality that transforms all her life.
>
> Now she has something real to get a grip on and to look forward to, and it changes her whole life. Every time she goes through a drugstore, she's looking for a bridal magazine; every time she passes a flower shop, she's thinking about the flowers she'll have. *Her whole life becomes preoccupied by the certainty of a future event that she anticipates.* Now that's biblical hope.
>
> God calls us to train our minds, our emotions, and our spirits on the certainty of the world to come. A world to come with its values, joys, and satisfaction can preoccupy our souls now. Just as a bride-to-be can have a tough day but say, "It's okay because the big day is coming," we can say the same thing in our lives when we have trained ourselves in the hope

of heaven and in the world to come. We're going to have tough days, but that's all right because the big day is yet to come.

Heaven is not "wouldn't that be nice." Heaven is reality. Christ rose from the dead to prove that life after death in a resurrected form is a reality for us.

Joseph Stowell

This Isn't Working

Some of you who are reading this may be thinking, *I already believe Christ died for my sins and that he's going to change the world someday, and I still feel as if there's no reason for hope or joy.* If that's how you feel, remember that in addition to personally accepting the implications of God's plan to change the world, you have to actively remind yourself of what God has done and what he's promised to do. One of the easiest ways to do this is to think about appropriate Scripture passages. Here are a few. Memorize them. Think about them throughout the day. Contemplate their meaning.

> For God so loved the world that he gave his one and only Son, that whoever believes in him shall not perish but have eternal life. (John 3:16)

> Christ was raised as the first of the harvest; then all who belong to Christ will be raised when he comes back.
> After that the end will come, when he will turn the Kingdom over to God the Father, having destroyed every ruler and authority and power. For Christ must reign until he humbles all his enemies beneath his feet. And the last enemy to be destroyed is death. (1 Cor. 15:23–26)

> No longer will there be any curse. . . . There will be no more night. They will not need the light of a lamp or the light of the sun, for the Lord God will give them light. And they will reign for ever and ever. The angel said to me, "These words are trustworthy and true." (Rev. 22:3, 5–6)

If reflecting on these things does not encourage you, examine whether you are placing your hope in something that can disappoint. If you're trusting in the next relationship, an event, the pain going away, or things getting back to normal, you're sure to be discouraged. All of those things are either impossible or temporary. They are not good candidates for you to place your hope in. As 1 Peter 1:13 says, seek to "set your hope on the grace to be brought to you."

If you discover that you are hoping in things that are fleeting, consider praying like the psalmist. He asks God to "turn my eyes from worthless things, and give me life through your word" (Ps. 119:37 NLT).

If Christ's work on the cross for you does not excite you, it could be that deep down you think you deserve God's mercy. Or you think that somehow, because of your faithfulness to God, you are earning favor with him. These mind-sets keep you from appreciating what God has done for you. Remember, the Bible teaches us that we were God's enemies and that his acceptance of us is a gift; it has nothing to do with our behavior (Eph. 2:1–9; Titus 3:5). When you realize that you don't deserve God's forgiveness and that only Christ's righteousness makes you acceptable to God, you'll delight more in your salvation.

> It's 3:00 a.m. and everything seems impossible. But there are words of Scripture that come through the centuries that can rescue us: "Thou wilt keep him in perfect peace, whose mind is stayed on thee" [Isa. 26:3 KJV]. Whenever my mind is really on Jesus, it can't be in turmoil; peace will come. The problem is learning how to stay our minds on Jesus, but there's a goal there, and we need to reach for it.
>
> Lorraine Peterson

A Word of Encouragement

You are grieving deeply because you loved deeply. But your grief does not have to dominate your life or cause you to become stuck in despair. Because of what Christ has done for you, you can grieve with joy. Because of what Christ will do for you, you can grieve with hope. You don't have to wait until you are over your grief to have hope and joy—you can have them now! As you look at God's promise of heaven, with no more tears and suffering, you can walk forward in the hopeful assurance that death is not the end for those who have trusted in Christ.

> He will swallow up death forever.
> The Sovereign LORD will wipe away the tears from all
>   faces. . . .
> In that day they will say,
>   "Surely this is our God;
>   we trusted in him, and he saved us." (Isa. 25:8–9)

Appendix A

Featured Experts

Throughout this book are wise insights and godly counsel from personal interviews with the following Christian experts:

Kay Arthur is a Bible teacher, the author of more than one hundred books and Bible studies, and a radio and television hostess. She experienced the death of her husband.

Susan Beeney, RN, an author and speaker on grief and loss, is the founder and executive director of New Hope Grief Support Community in Southern California.

Dr. Richard Bewes, a son of English missionaries in East Africa, was rector of All Souls Church in London, England, for over twenty years. He is a well-known speaker on many continents and has written numerous books.

Sabrina Black is an international speaker and professional counselor. She is the CEO and clinical director of Abundant Life Counseling Center in Detroit, Michigan, and has authored/coauthored several books. She experienced the loss of her uncle, sister-in-law, and father-in-law and the miscarriage of her baby.

Judy Blore is the director of BASIS, a ministry of Handi* Vangelism, which provides help for bereaved parents and their families in southeastern Pennsylvania. She experienced the death of her mother.

The late **Dr. Bill Bright** was the founder and president of Campus Crusade for Christ. For over fifty years, he dedicated his life to helping people find new life and hope through a relationship with Christ.

Dr. Tim Clinton is the president of the executive board for the American Association of Christian Counselors (AACC). He authored *Caring for People God's Way: Personal and Emotional Issues, Addictions, Grief, and Trauma*. His father passed away.

Dr. Larry Crabb is a psychologist, conference speaker, Bible teacher, and author. He is the founder and director of NewWay Ministries. Dr. Crabb is the spiritual director for the AACC. His books include *Shattered Dreams* and *The Safest Place on Earth*. He experienced the death of his brother.

Dr. Robert DeVries and **Dr. Susan Zonnebelt-Smeenge** have both experienced the death of a spouse. Now remarried to each other, they work together to help people who are grieving. Dr. DeVries is a professor of church education (emeritus) at Calvin Theological Seminary. Dr. Zonnebelt-Smeenge is a licensed clinical psychologist having recently retired from Pine Rest Christian Mental Health Services. They speak internationally and are joint authors of several books and articles, including *Getting to the Other Side of Grief*; *The Empty Chair: Handling Grief on Holidays and Special Occasions*; *Living Fully in the Shadow of Death*; *Traveling through Grief*; and *From We to Me*.

Joni Eareckson Tada is the founder and president of Joni and Friends Ministries. Her books and worldwide ministry reflect her experience of God's love and grace since becoming a quadriplegic over thirty-five years ago. Her books include *Heaven* and *When God Weeps*.

Elisabeth Elliot, born of missionary parents, served as a missionary in Ecuador, where the Auca Indians killed her husband, Jim Elliot, in 1956. She also experienced the death of her second husband. She is a speaker and the author of numerous books, including *A Path through Suffering, Facing the Death of Someone You Love,* and *The Path of Loneliness.*

Anne Graham Lotz is a speaker and the president/CEO of AnGeL Ministries. The daughter of Billy and Ruth Graham, Anne hosts Just Give Me Jesus revivals throughout the world. She has authored several books, including *Heaven: My Father's House.* Anne experienced her mother's death.

David and Nancy Guthrie are cohosts of the GriefShare® support group program video. David is an executive in the church music publishing industry. Nancy is an author and Bible teacher, and she runs her own media relations firm. Nancy has authored *Holding On to Hope* and *The One Year Book of Hope.* They faced the loss of two infant children.

The late **Barbara Johnson**, who lost two sons and her husband, was involved in grief ministry. A humorous writer and speaker, she also headed Spatula Ministries in La Habra, California, supporting parents who lost children through death or estrangement. Her many books include *Splashes of Joy in the Cesspools of Life* and *God's Most Precious Jewels Are Crystallized Tears.*

Dr. Robert Kellemen is a licensed professional clinical counselor and the director of the Biblical Counseling and Spiritual Formation Network of the AACC. He is also the author of *God's Healing for Life's Losses.* On his twenty-first birthday, he experienced his father's death.

Dr. Tim Lane is the president of the Christian Counseling and Educational Foundation (CCEF) in Glenside, Pennsylvania. He is an author and served as a pastor for ten years. His younger brother died at forty-two after a twenty-five-year struggle with addictions.

Sue Lutz served as a counselor at CCEF for fourteen years. Now she counsels at her church, where her husband serves as pastor. She authored the booklet *Thankfulness: Even When It Hurts*. Susan experienced the loss of both parents.

Dr. Norman Peart is the founder and pastor of Grace Bible Fellowship in Cary, North Carolina. He is also a professor at the University of North Carolina at Chapel Hill. Dr. Peart experienced the loss of his grandmother.

Lorraine Peterson, author of *Restore My Soul*, currently resides in Mexico, where she works with young people and ministers to those who have experienced the death of a loved one. She experienced the death of her mother and stepmother.

Laura Petherbridge is an international author and speaker who serves singles and couples through topics such as relationships, spiritual growth, and divorce prevention and recovery.

Dr. David Powlison, editor of the *Journal of Biblical Counseling*, is a counselor and faculty member at CCEF and the author of *Seeing with New Eyes: Counseling and the Human Condition through the Lens of Scripture* and other books.

Dr. Ray Pritchard is a conference speaker and the president of Keep Believing Ministries. He has ministered extensively overseas. Dr. Pritchard has authored several books, including *Why Did This Happen to Me?* His father passed away.

Lois Rabey is a speaker at churches, conferences, crusades, and on television/radio programs, and she is the author of numerous books, including *When Your Soul Aches* and *Moments for Those Who Have Lost a Loved One*. She experienced the loss of her husband.

Winston Smith is the director of counseling, a counselor, and a faculty member at CCEF, and a lecturer in practical theology at Westminster Theological Seminary.

Dr. Joseph Stowell was the president of the Moody Bible Institute of Chicago for eighteen years and is the current president of Cornerstone University in Grand Rapids, Michigan. Dr. Stowell is an internationally recognized speaker and the author of *Eternity* and other books.

Dr. **Siang-Yang Tan** is a professor of psychology at Fuller Theological Seminary. He is the senior pastor of First Evangelical Church Glendale in California and has authored many publications, including *Coping with Depression* (coauthored with John Ortberg). His father passed away.

Dr. **John Trent**, a nationally recognized author and speaker, is the president of StrongFamilies and the Center for StrongFamilies in Scottsdale, Arizona. He experienced the loss of his mother and father.

Dr. **Paul Tripp** is the president of Paul Tripp Ministries and the author of several books on practical issues of Christian living, including *A Shelter in the Time of Storm*. He is on the pastoral staff of Tenth Presbyterian Church in Philadelphia and has been a counselor for many years. He experienced his father's death.

Dr. **Edward Welch** is a counselor and faculty member at CCEF and a professor of practical theology at Westminster Theological Seminary. He has authored several books, such as *Depression: A Stubborn Darkness*, and he speaks at conferences and other venues. His father passed away.

H. Norman Wright is a grief therapist and certified trauma specialist. He is the author of over seventy books, including *Experiencing Grief, Recovering from Losses in Life*, and *It's Okay to Cry*. He is on the faculty of Talbot Graduate School of Theology and on the executive board of the AACC. He experienced the death of his son and wife.

Zig Ziglar is a motivational speaker and the author of twenty-seven books, including *Confessions of a Grieving Christian*, which is based on the grief journey he experienced after the loss of his daughter, Suzan Witmeyer. He is chair of the Zig Ziglar Corporation, whose mission is to equip people to utilize their physical, mental, and spiritual resources.

Appendix B

GriefShare®: Help for Those in Grief

We encourage you to find a GriefShare® grief recovery support group near you. At GriefShare® you will find practical help and tools to move forward through your grief. You will meet people who can truly relate to how you are feeling and to the situations you are now facing. You'll find real comfort, solid support, and biblical help.

What Does a Typical GriefShare® Meeting Look Like?

At a GriefShare® meeting, you'll view a video featuring people on the path of healing after a loved one's death, Christian experts on grief-related topics, and short dramas on living with grief. After the video, you will be part of a group that discusses the video teaching and how you can apply what you've learned over the next week. You'll also have the opportunity to share concerns, questions, and prayer requests.

During the days between meetings, you will work through a workbook that contains additional insights on grief, questions to answer about your grief, a helpful weekly Bible study, and a weekly journal to help you sort through your emotions and track your healing progress.

Find a GriefShare® Group Near You

GriefShare® groups are located across the US, Canada, and in other countries. To find a list of groups near you, visit www.griefshare.org. Look for the "Find a Group" search box, enter the requested information, and discover a list of nearby groups. You can also call 800-395-5755 or 919-562-2112 to find a group in your area.

Visit GriefShare® Online

The GriefShare® website provides helpful information and resources for people in the midst of grief. At www.griefshare.org, you'll discover:

- where to find the nearest GriefShare® group
- recommended books and resources dealing with grief recovery and specific grief-related topics
- a free year of encouraging daily email messages for those in grief
- a free, downloadable personal Bible study
- articles and video clips on how to survive the holidays after a loss
- advice on how to start a GriefShare® group
- more about the GriefShare® ministry and Church Initiative, Inc., which sponsors GriefShare®

More Church Initiative Care Programs

GriefShare®'s parent ministry is Church Initiative, Inc., an organization that assists churches in establishing support groups and teaching groups for people dealing with life crises and other life issues. Other Church Initiative care groups and programs include:

- DivorceCare®, divorce recovery support groups for people hurting from the pain of separation and divorce (www.divorcecare.org)
- DivorceCare® for Kids™, help for children whose parents are separated or divorced (www.dc4k.org)
- Choosing Wisely: Before You Divorce™, a marriage crisis counseling strategy (www.beforeyoudivorce.org)
- Chance to Change™, Christ-centered gambling addiction recovery support groups (www.chancetochange.org)
- Single & Parenting™, practical help and encouragement for single parents (www.singleandparenting.org)

To find the above care groups that are meeting in your area, call 800-395-5755 or email info@churchinitiative.org.

Samuel J. Hodges IV is executive producer for Church Initiative. He graduated from Howard University with a degree in communications. After that, he received a Master of Divinity degree from Southeastern Baptist Theological Seminary with an emphasis in Christian education. After graduating, Sam joined Church Initiative and wrote and/or produced a number of their video-based, small group curriculums (GriefShare®, Chance to Change™, Facing Forever™, and Single and Parenting™). For two years, Sam also served on staff as a discipleship pastor at Infinity Church in Laurel, Maryland.

Sam is married to Rachel, whom he met at a Howard University Campus Crusade for Christ meeting. They have four children: Katrina, Sam, Nadia, and Amber. Sam enjoys playing basketball, teaching his family, watching movies, rooting for the Washington Wizards and Redskins, and playing with his children.

Kathy Leonard is editorial director for Church Initiative. Kathy has been writing and editing for over twenty years. After graduating with an English degree from the University of Maryland Asian Division in Okinawa, Japan, Kathy moved with her Air Force husband, Tim, to England. There she wrote feature articles for the Air Force base newspaper and worked as a publicist/graphic designer for the 48th Services Squadron. In 2000, Church Initiative hired her as a writer and editor.

Because of her time spent at Church Initiative, Kathy has developed a passion to minister to people in life crises through her writings. She is coauthor of *Through a Season of Grief: Devotions for Your Journey from Mourning to Joy* and *Divorce Care: Hope, Help, and Healing during and after Your Divorce*.

Kathy and her husband, Tim, live in Palmyra, Virginia, with their three children, Jacob, Alanna, and Luke. Kathy enjoys reading, cooking, dancing, and spending time with family and friends.

Let God EMBRACE you
in the MIDST of GRIEF

You can *still* live life to the *fullest*

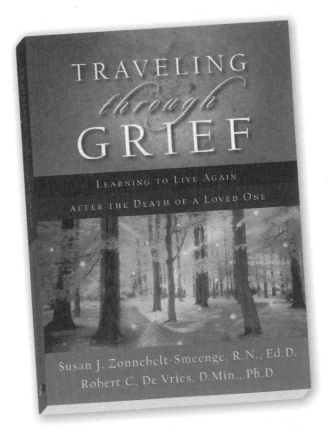

How to handle holidays and special occasions without your loved one

The Empty Chair

HANDLING GRIEF *on* HOLIDAYS
and SPECIAL OCCCASIONS

SUSAN J. ZONNEBELT-SMEENGE, R.N., ED.D.
and ROBERT C. DE VRIES, D.MIN., PH.D.

Help for Those in Grief

We encourage you to find a GriefShare grief recovery support group program near you. At GriefShare you will find practical help and tools to move forward through your grief. You will meet people who can truly relate to how you are feeling and to the situations you are now facing. You'll find real comfort, solid support, and biblical help.

FIND A GRIEFSHARE GROUP NEAR YOU

GriefShare groups are located across the United States and Canada and in other countries. To find a list of groups near you, visit www.griefshare. org. Look for the "Find a Group" search box, enter the requested information, and discover a list of nearby groups. You can also call 800-395-5755 or 919-562-2112 to find a group in your area.

VISIT GRIEFSHARE ONLINE

GriefShare.org provides helpful information and resources for people in the midst of grief. Visit us at www.griefshare.org.